POSTCARDS

POSTCARDS

The Rise and Fall
of the
World's First
Social Network

LYDIA PYNE

REAKTION BOOKS

To Stan and Esther
And to Karlie, Ashley, Lindsey, Colten, Julie, and Ivy

Published by
REAKTION BOOKS LTD
Unit 32, Waterside
44–48 Wharf Road
London N1 7UX, UK
www.reaktionbooks.co.uk

First published 2021
Copyright © Lydia Pyne 2021

Printed and bound in India by Replika Press Pvt. Ltd

A catalogue record for this book is available from the British Library

ISBN 978 1 78914 484 0

CONTENTS

INTRODUCTION:
INVENTION AND REINVENTION *7*

ONE
SIGNED, STAMPED, AND DELIVERED *19*

TWO
THE MEANS OF MASS PRODUCTION *51*

THREE
PUBLICITY AND PROPAGANDA *83*

FOUR
HAVING A WONDERFUL TIME, WISH YOU WERE HERE *115*

FIVE
POSTCARDS FROM COUNTRIES THAT NO LONGER EXIST *151*

CONCLUSION:
THE AFTERLIVES OF POSTCARDS *187*

REFERENCES *205*

BIBLIOGRAPHY *218*

ACKNOWLEDGMENTS *224*

PHOTO ACKNOWLEDGMENTS *226*

INDEX *228*

INTRODUCTION:
INVENTION AND REINVENTION

....

Postcards are personal.

This will come as no surprise to anyone who has ever sent or received one. ("Saw this and thought of you!" "Wish you were here!" "Can't wait to see you!" "This is a picture of the hotel where we're staying, and the beach looks just like the postcard!") Short, sweet, and to the point—postcards simply don't have the space for a sender to scrawl anything more than a couple of lines.

But a postcard is much more than just what's written on its back. Postcards carry messages in myriad ways—through the pictures that are printed on them, the machinery of their mass manufacture, and the networks that facilitate their journey through the mail. Written communication via postcard might be short and simple, but postcards themselves are deceptively complex objects and the stuff of the first worldwide social network. Ultimately, postcards connect people with geographies and, in turn, geographies with people.

Historians estimate that in the first two decades of the twentieth century something like 200 billion postcards were in global circulation. Centuries of various print technologies meant postcards could easily be mass-produced, but it was millennia of social infrastructure that ensured they could be sent and delivered around the world.[1]

"Greeting from Monterey, Mex." "Greetings from" quickly became
a mainstay of postcard designs around the world. Unmailed postcard,
Ward Bros, Columbus, Ohio, c. 1890s.

Postcards were unendingly popular almost as soon as they were
invented in the mid-nineteenth century, reaching their commercial peak
just before the First World War. A large part of what made postcards
such an enduring medium was—is!—a material, tangible connection
between people. ("The sender wrote out this message, they addressed
it, they stuck a stamp on it. Then they sent it to me.") This physical
connection between sender and recipient can't be found in any other
sort of mass-printed medium.

"There are stories of Soviet prisoners receiving postcards while they
were in exile in the 1920s and '30s," historian Alison Rowley pointed
to by way of a historical example as she and I talked about her research
into postcards from the Russian Revolution. "Prisoners could receive
postcards, even when other kinds of written communications like letters were not allowed. Prisoners would stroke the handwriting on the

postcards, tracing words and letters, because it was a physical connection to the sender."[2]

From the transatlantic women's suffrage movements, to emerging middle-class tourism, to the nascent photojournalism of the early 1900s, to the postcards sent and received today, postcards cultivate personal connections, linking people across the globe one picture at a time.

. . . .

Postcards are also about storytelling. Although many early to mid-nineteenth-century postcards (then called "post cards," "private mailing cards," or "postal cards") were printed without images, pictures quickly became an integral part of what people would come to consider an archetypical or "proper" postcard. If a picture is worth a thousand words, it's guaranteed that the images on picture postcards have long

"Greetings from South Carolina." Iconic Americana postcard design printed by Curt Teich & Co., c. 1938.

said more than could be crammed into the message space on the back. Postcards offered an easy, immediate, and visual story.

What kinds of images have made their way onto postcards over the years? In short, anything and everything. Charming and quaint landscapes were—are!—popular motifs, as were—are!—formal portraits of famous or important people. Images of buildings, cities, or engineering feats offer a validation of civic or national projects. Postcards boast satirical cartoons, business advertisements, and political propaganda. Some are printed with maps and national borders clearly demarcated. Some are simple ink sketches. There are saucy photographs of scantily clad ladies and not so saucy family photographs; historically, insufferably saccharine pouty-faced Kewpie kids were insanely popular (American postcards of the 1910s, I'm looking at you.) And, of course, postcards with holiday greetings. You name it, and I am willing to bet that it can be found on a postcard.

"Some of the images that I've come across on postcards are really just . . . banal," librarian Raymond Khan of the New York Public Library Picture Collection said as he introduced me to the library's massive collection of postcards. "I look at some of them and think, 'A flowerpot? Really? You put a flowerpot on a postcard?'" He shook his head. "But, of course, there are the serious postcards, too."[3]

Although anything and everything can and has been put on a postcard, there are certain image trends and patterns that are particularly good at telling stories and that resonate with buyers, senders, and recipients. Some popular postcard genres became ways for turn-of-the-twentieth-century emerging countries to create national narratives through pictures of architecture or building projects (iconic bridges, for example) that are inexorably tied to national identity. Counter-revolutionaries could command a media presence that fell outside official state channels. Social movements could gain popular traction through postcards.

Somewhat counterintuitively, the more one looks through thousands of postcards—all telling their different stories—the more predictable and samey these postcard images start to seem. Is this predictability of postcard pictures any wonder, really, for those of us posting the twenty-first century's equivalent of digital postcards via Instagram, where we see a certain aesthetic "sameness" emerge? "Instagram . . . has its own aesthetic language," *New Yorker* cultural critic Jia Tolentino observed. "The aesthetic is also marked by a familiar human aspiration . . . toward a generic sameness . . . Some things just perform well."[4]

There's a certain comfort in the aesthetic predictability of what we'll see and how we'll see it. And the consumption of media images—Instagram and postcards alike—acts like a feedback loop, ensuring that what's popular is, well, popular. As it turns out, the idea that "some things just perform well"—that we simply gravitate toward a certain aesthetic expectation for certain types of images—isn't a bad way to think about how certain types of picture postcards come in and out of fashion, particularly during the early twentieth century, when postcards were sent around the world by the billion.

. . . .

Postcards have been printed, sold, mailed, and received on a scale that makes them, historically, the largest class of artifacts that humankind has ever exchanged.

There are a lot of different ways to dig into the history of postcards and any history will inevitably be incomplete. Although postcards were a mass medium, they were—and still are—a disposable one. This disposability means that there are holes in the historical record, making a complete archive of all the world's postcards inherently impossible. Many histories of postcards opt to explore postcards through specific pictorial or geographic themes ("historic postcards of New York City") or printed types ("American holiday postcards.") These narrow, specific approaches tend to focus on postcards by a particular manufacturer, such as the iconic Curt Teich & Co. Americana postcards or the carefully lithographed portraits found on cards by London printer

Partial View of City, looking West,
Austin, Texas.

Postcard from Austin, Texas. Wear and tear speak to the postcard's handling over the last
hundred years. Mailed in 1915 to "Mr. Robert Boles, Buck Meadows, California."

Raphael Tuck & Sons. Others opt to concentrate on specific postcard technologies, like Kodak's "real picture" postcards. As many types and styles as there are of postcards, there is an equal number of ways to talk about their histories.

This book offers a different sort of postcard story. Rather than zero in on a specific subset of postcard images to illustrate cultural or visual histories, I've opted to focus on the material life of postcards as tangible, social, and personal objects. *Postcards* is about the life cycle of postcards and the networks that built them; it's a collection of themes about print culture, tourism, propaganda, technologies, and the afterlives of artifacts all told through postcards. To understand postcards, I think, requires us to consider everything from cuneiform tablets to printed indulgences—to look at postal systems, photography, propaganda, and historical geography. When we look at a postcard, we're looking at a sum of decisions made over thousands of years about communication, technology, and how to match a message to a medium. These are all tools that built the medium of postcards.

This wide-ranging approach offers, I hope, a new way to unpack how global networks are built as well as the technological and social infrastructure that goes into their development and maintenance. I've tried to include some episodes that feature classic postcards and notable postcard manufactures as well as small anecdotes from individual postcards that I've come across in my research and writing. I'd like to think that such examples highlight the myriad postcards, senders, and recipients that history has seen over the last century and a half.

Throughout this project, I've learned at first hand that postcards are personal and always have been. I didn't start out to write a book that drew so heavily from collections of family postcards or to highlight my

Postcard with pre-printed message to its recipients, subtly shaming them for missing Sunday school. Short-run, pre-printed postcards like this were popular alternatives to mailed letters. Mailed in 1914, Iowa.

own different postcard experiences. But, completely unexpectedly, the medium lent itself to this approach, as postcards require us to recognize that global social networks are built out of individual stories and connections. The more I dug into stories about postcards, the more I found myself and my family in them.

For example, my own great-grandfather, Robert Boles, saved a shoebox full of hundreds of postcards that were sent to him between 1905 and 1920—what historians call the Golden Age of Postcards. His daughter, my grandmother, kept the cards for years and gave them to my mom, who has long been interested in family history from my dad's side of the family. My mom bequeathed the postcards to me when I started the background research for *Postcards*, convinced that these family mementos would offer a way to humanize the global postcard phenomenon. She was right.

As I sorted through the shoebox, I found that most of Great-grandfather Robert's postcards dated to the early 1910s, mailed to him by family and friends back in Oklahoma. (His father, Alfred Boles, was a lawyer and, later, a judge. Robert kept some postcards that advertised Alfred's law practice.) Some of these postcards offered cutesy pictures, some seasonal greetings. Many were images of buildings from different downtowns, capitalizing on a small-town Americana vibe. A few had outright racist or misogynistic illustrated memes with 1911 snark scrawled in the message space. The shoebox collection turned out to be a mini time capsule that illustrated just about every type of postcard printing technology and almost every reason why people sent and received postcards at the turn of the twentieth century. Working through family collections of postcards helped hone my sense of what I wanted to look for in bigger institutional collections.

To that end, reading postcards in various libraries and archives felt a bit as though I was reading messages in bottles; I didn't know the recipient or the sender, and the message on the back would have made sense only to them. To put it another way, it was like reading a stranger's text messages and trying to figure out the backstory for any individual text. Drawing on postcards from my family's collection meant that I "knew" the people writing, receiving, or saving the postcards in a way that I couldn't with postcards from other institutional collections. It continued to make postcards personal.

Such collections of family postcards aren't exceptional, and postcards are tucked into nooks and crannies all over the world. "Why do so many people have collections of postcards that have been moved through attics, cupboards, and garage sales to their curious owners today?" historian Daniel Gifford ponders in *American Holiday Postcards, 1905–1915*.[5] Gifford credits his family's own shoebox collections of postcards with originally piquing his research interest into the history of holiday postcards. "I didn't realize it at the time, but my great-grandmother's collection would give me a window into the desires—and anxieties—of a world I would only later come to understand and appreciate as I pursued my doctorate in American history," he notes. "Until I embarked on that journey, the cards often sat in the back of closets or under piles of other accumulated stuff."[6]

My collection of family postcards has long outgrown the shoebox I originally started out with, especially once word of the project spread. When I mentioned to older family members that I was working on this book, the invariable response was, "Oh, I have some postcards saved in a box somewhere. Let me send them to you." And send them they did. As relatives have cleaned out attics, cupboards, garages, and closets to find their old postcards, I have watched my burgeoning collection grow. Everyone who sent along postcards told me how glad they were that they were going to a "good cause." Here, at the end of writing this book, it turns out that I am now the official family Keeper of Postcards in Shoeboxes.

. . . .

"Postcards? You're writing a book about postcards? Does anyone still send postcards anymore?" I am unvaryingly asked when I talk about this project. The short answer to this question is, "Nope. People sure don't."

Correspondenz-Karten from Austria were the first postcards to be formalized as a class of mail and a type of correspondence. This example was mailed on October 22, 1870, and arrived the next day.

"Photochrom" postcard from Constantinople and the Sea of Marmora, Turkey. The "photochrom" process allowed printers to create a colorized image from a black-and-white photographic negative; negatives were transferred directly onto lithographic printing plates to be printed on a large, commercial scale. Printed 1890–1900, Detroit Publishing Co.

But people sure did. Over the past hundred and fifty years, postcards have flooded every sort of market and have been sent and received at a rate that is unmatched in any sort of history of human communication. When postcards (called *Correspondenz-Karten*) went into circulation in Austria on October 1, 1869, nearly 3 million were sold in the first three months alone. Just over 90 million postcards (called *открытое письмо*, "open letters" or, more commonly, *cartes postales*, as they were in Europe) were mailed in Russia in 1900. A mere decade later, that figure had increased to 337.3 million a year. Historians estimate that more than a billion postcards passed through the German postal system alone in 1903. Throughout the nineteenth and twentieth centuries, printers developed new ink and cardstock technologies to be able to put more postcards in front of more people, at the price that audiences expected. (And that price was, in a word, "cheap.")[7] Postcards were legion.

In the twenty-first century, postcards can feel rather quaint, like artifacts from an era when a postal system signified something other than Amazon Prime delivery. But postcards established a social expectation that one ought to be able to send inexpensive messages around the world. This expectation hasn't changed in the past century—it's just the material and infrastructure that have. "In the 1990s the advent of e-cards and email started the decline of the postcard's popularity," the Smithsonian Institute suggests. "Today postcards are typically purchased as souvenirs, rather than a quick way to communicate."[8] Reading between the Smithsonian's lines, it's easy to conclude that postcards have basically gone extinct in the wild as a print medium.

The short answer to "Do people still send postcards?" is "No." But this isn't the full story. People don't send them at the rate they did in the past, but they do still send them. (For example, postcards were a popular medium with which to encourage American voters to vote in the 2016 and 2020 elections.) Moreover, postcards have taken on a unique afterlife as a popular and enduring medium for artists and collectors alike. As such, postcards continue to circulate, just not always—or only—through the post, as they once did. Historic postcards are recirculated through art and media and consistently used as visual proxies for decades past. Even if someone has never sent or received a postcard, there's a sense of what the postcard medium "ought" to do.

Postcards have left an indelible imprint on the history of human communication, unmatched by any other material medium. They owe their success to the decentralization of their manufacture as well as the physical material connection they created between sender and recipient. Postcards and their digital descendants continue to be about personal connections—specifically, short, cheap, ephemeral messages. There are inexorable echoes of postcards in contemporary digital picture networks such as Instagram, Twitter, Facebook, Snapchat, TikTok, and other photo-sharing apps. We recreate old social networks—old postcard social lines, if you will—with every post of a digital picture. Postcards are not yet completely extinct.

ONE

SIGNED, STAMPED,
AND DELIVERED

....

I n 1909 the United States Post Office was in crisis. When it closed its books on June 30 of that year, it was $17 million in the red, with no hope of digging itself out of its financial hole.

The $17 million shortfall was a considerable sum of money. Only eleven years earlier, the United States had paid $20 million to Spain to cede Guam, Puerto Rico, and the sovereignty of the Philippines to the United States after signing the Treaty of Paris on December 10, 1898. In other words, the Post Office Department's 1909 deficit was on par with what other departments in the U.S. government were spending to wrap up the three-month-long Spanish-American War. (Today the Post Office's $17 million deficit would be equivalent to $483 million when adjusted for inflation.) "At the time, it was the largest deficit ever recorded by the department," historian Daniel Gifford relates, "and investigations, recrimination, and proposed solutions began almost immediately."[1]

But a mere two years later, on June 30, 1911, the Post Office announced that it could report a surplus of just over $200,000, which is just over $5.7 million today. What happened?

In a word: Postcards.

"Greetings from New York" printed by Theodor Eismann. This postcard was printed in 1909, the year postcards offered the United States Post Office a way out of potential bankruptcy.

By the turn of the twentieth century, postcards were a massive industry. Hundreds of billions of postcards were made, bought, sent, and delivered around the world. The popularity of postcards in the United States grew, as it did around the globe, and the number of postcards Americans sent and received roughly doubled between 1909 and 1911. Rural and urban dwellers alike sent hundreds of millions of postcards, making the industry incredibly lucrative at a time when the Post Office badly needed Americans to have a reason to mail more items.

"It requires an average of 120 post cards to weigh a pound, and thus the Post Office Department receives $1.20 a pound for carrying post cards, as against an average of transportation of 9 or 10 cents a pound," *Washington Post* columnist Frederic Haskin wrote in his analysis of the American postal crisis in 1910. "The post card business is very profitable to the Post Office."[2]

Although postcard postage revenue helped tip the budget toward its 1911 surplus, there was still the question of how the Post Office had gotten itself into the situation to begin with. "Recent investigations have shown that the two great sources of loss to the postal revenues are second-class mail matter and rural delivery. The loss on second-class mail matter has been increasing for many years until it now amounts to more than $64,000,000," American Postmaster General Frank Hitchcock declared in 1909. "The loss from rural delivery, a service begun hardly a dozen years ago, and of unprecedented growth, reaches nearly $28,000,000."[3]

In other words, the initial financial crisis could be attributed to the geography of the United States as well as the physical items that people were mailing. Getting mail to rural-living Americans was costing the Post Office more per item than urban post.

More than four decades earlier, in 1863, the United States Congress had approved free home delivery for cities that met population and economic requirements. A city had to have a population of 10,000 individuals and $10,000 in gross postal receipts (equivalent to $205,000 today) to justify the cost of door-to-door, hand-delivered service. Nineteenth- to early-twentieth-century mail deliveries were made Monday to Friday, several times a day, quickly putting the Postal Service under intense economic pressure to deliver mail to places it hadn't previously serviced and to do it on a predictable, reliable schedule. In the city of Baltimore, for example, a letter carrier could visit up to seven times a day in 1905. By 1923, however, delivery was streamlined to the traditional once-a-day delivery schedule. That same year, requirements were set down that new homes must have a box or slot for mail, thus making delivery more efficient, as carriers wouldn't have to wait around for hand deliveries to be accepted.[4]

Delivering mail to cities and towns was one thing. Delivering mail to scattered rural populations and hamlets in the mid-nineteenth century, however, was something else altogether. In rural areas, where the U.S. government did not offer free delivery, private mail delivery companies

Rural mail carrier in early electric automobile at mailboxes, c. 1910.

filled in the demand. It wasn't until 1893, when Georgia Congressman Thomas E. Watson pushed the legislation through, that Rural Free Delivery—free delivery outside of cities and towns—became a mandated service. By 1896, Rural Free Delivery had expanded even further to include residences that were difficult to reach. Yet some areas were so remote that daily mail proved impossible—delivery to the indigenous Havasupai community at the bottom of the Grand Canyon, for example, was limited to three times a week.

Those who delivered letters and periodicals along those newly developed rural routes put in some serious miles. By 1901 the total mileage traveled by carriers on Free Rural Delivery had increased to over 100,000 miles, the cost of the service was something like $1.75 million, and it employed over 37,000 carriers. Those numbers did nothing but increase, and nine years later, 40,997 carriers traveled 993,068 miles, costing the Post Office Department $36,915,000 (just over $1 billion today.) This service fast became an expectation for rural Americans. Even more quickly, however, Rural Free Delivery became a drain on postal resources.[5]

Testifying before a House subcommittee in 1908, Postmaster General George Meyer suggested, "it seems that the rural delivery, while not strictly self-sustaining, does add largely to the receipts. In other words, the correspondence comes from the centers to the people in the rural deliveries, and that is credited to the large post-offices."[6] By 1909 the Post Office was in such dire straits that it considered simply suspending rural deliveries as a cost-saving measure. The backlash to that proposal was immediate and intense—Americans were having none of it.

At the same time as delivery options were being negotiated, the Post Office officially recognized six classes of mail, including postcards. Between 1905 and 1909, the amount of mail delivered in rural areas vastly exceeded the amount that was sent. But "postcard class" showed an increase in what was collected versus what was delivered along rural routes, the only class of mail to do so. Specifically, between 1905 and 1909, there was a 410 percent increase in postcards delivered to rural routes, and an 846 percent increase in the number of cards collected from those same routes. More postcards were being sent from these places than were delivered to them. The social pattern indicates that idyllic, non-urban landscapes were places to visit and to write home about, but were not, perhaps, places where the majority of Americans lived.

Postcards thus defied the American rural-urban cultural divide and became a lifeline for the Post Office. Americans sent postcards and, more to the point, they sent a lot of them. To that end, "rural Americans were circulating an idealized vision of themselves,"Gifford suggests. "When times seemed tough, all those picture-perfect fields, barns, fences, and country homes became a way to create an alternative narrative—one that was beautiful, healthy, and prosperous."[7] Between June 1907 and June 1908 Americans mailed 667 million postcards in the United States. (Specifically, Christmas of 1908 saw 2 million postcards overwhelm Brooklyn's post office and substations and 1909 rang in with full postcard fervor.[8]) Based on the 1910 census numbers, Gifford calculates that would average out to something like "seven postcards a year for every man, woman, and child in the nation, and that does not even count postcards collected in albums and boxes and never mailed."[9]

In short, between 1909 and 1911, Americans were sending postcards at unprecedented rates. The popularity of postcards might have come as a shock to Post Office Department accountants—who counted and tallied the hundreds of millions of pieces of mail sent each year—but it was no surprise to the merchants who sold Americans their postcards. A postcard dealer from Waterloo, Iowa, wrote in 1909, "We have tried for a long time to drum it into the heads of the producers of post cards that a majority of the business is done in country towns."[10]

The postcard craze arrived at an opportune moment as a unique solution to the Post Office's financial crisis. Although Americans had been sending and receiving postcards since the mid-nineteenth century, new types of postcards began to emerge and with them, new technologies for mass production and new expectations about buying and sending them. "It was rural and country town Americans who, through their embrace of a popular fad [postcards], built a lifeline to a struggling Post Office Department," Gifford contends. "It was a lifeline built one postcard at a time."[11] Postcards created enough revenue to turn a deficit into a surplus for the Post Office and simultaneously ended discussion of halting daily rural deliveries.

Interestingly—and perhaps unsurprisingly—1909 was hardly the first time that the Postal Service was at the edge of financial solvency, nor would it be the last. (In 1847, for example, the Post Office's financial fiasco was mitigated when postage began to be charged to the sender, rather than collected from the recipient. This change met with outrage when it was first implemented, but quickly became the new normal for sending letters through the American post.) Postcards, however, were enough to stave off the 1909 financial catastrophe for the United States Postal Service for fourteen years.

Graustark will be here Nov. 5,
Friday and I am simply wild.

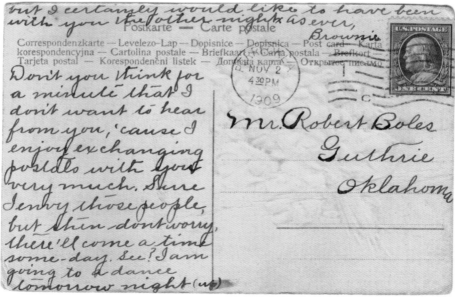

but I certainly would like to have been
with you the other night. as ever,
Brownie

Don't you think for
a minute that I
don't want to hear
from you, 'cause I
enjoy exchanging
postals with you
very much. Sure
I envy those people,
but then don't worry,
there'll come a time
some-day. See? I am
going to a dance
tomorrow night (up)

Mr. Robert Boles
Guthrie
Oklahoma

Front and back of postcard to Robert Boles from his sister Marjorie ("Brownie.")
The message extends onto the front of the card. Mailed 1909.

Across the Atlantic, sending postcards played an equally important role in the social fabric of the UK. The Royal Mail sold 833 million stamps for postcards in 1909, or nearly twenty each for every man, woman, and child in the country. Historical estimates suggest that 6 billion postcards passed through the Royal Mail between 1902 and 1910, connecting colonial outposts with the British Empire's metropoles as well as connecting people to each other domestically. There wasn't anything unique about the American craze for postcards: It was being played out in countries all around the world.[12]

. . . .

"Picture postcards were more than just a means of communication; they provided a portrait of life in America, especially life in the first two decades of the twentieth century. Postcards were produced for every occasion," Senior Librarian Fred Bassett of the New York State Library Manuscripts and Special Collections explains. "At a time when newspapers (especially in small towns) carried few if any photographs, the postcard offered an incredibly inexpensive and convenient way to capture people, places, and events."[13]

Americans—again, like everyone around the globe—were sending millions and millions of postcards at the turn of the twentieth century. It is easy to simply see postcards as an ephemeral mass medium and forget that each card bought and sent was a connection between two people. When the historical network of postcards was built by the billions, individual cards don't seem to matter. Taking the time to read through the minutiae of what warranted being written and sent on a postcard, however, becomes a way of putting names to messages and bringing stories to life.

Thanks to my shoebox collection of family postcards, I could read through hundreds of messages to Robert Boles that had been saved. Postcards were addressed to Robert as "Bob," "Bobbie," or "Kid." (Robert moved to Redlands, California, after growing up in Oklahoma. He worked as a land surveyor in the Bay Area.) Postcards from Oklahoma came from friends, family, and colleagues that he knew before his move. They offered a day-to-day perspective that made the billions of postcards circulating around the world real in a way that postcards from archives—without specific context or stories attached—hadn't.

Robert's cards fit every genre and motif of postcard art and were everything that every postcard historian has described of postcards from the Golden Age. I came across one postcard requesting an invitation to a dance. A reminder of a change of address. Wishing a co-worker a Very Merry Christmas. A card from a trip to Mount Shasta. Postcards from family members asking why he hadn't written. ("Have been waiting for weeks for a letter, think you are real mean.") Some had just a name signed on the back. There were pictures of town squares and national parks, and enough garishly colored postcards of buildings in Perry, Oklahoma, that I'm pretty sure I could re-create the town's architecture from that time period if necessary. (Perry is located roughly 60 miles north of Oklahoma City, just east of the I-35 interstate.) There were cartoon messages that alternated between insipidly smug and outright offensive.

Since 1909 was such a crucial moment in United States Post Office history, I sifted through Robert's cards to find any that were postmarked from that year. There were only a couple; most were from 1911 and later, when his travel for work picked up.

One of the 1909 postcards in Robert's collection was a linen-printed one featuring a bouquet of purple forget-me-nots with the phrase "A Pure and Tender Thought" on the front; the back was labeled "postcard" in sixteen different languages, with space on the left-hand side for a message and lines on the right for a mailing address. "Don't you think for a minute that I don't want to hear from you, 'cause I enjoy exchanging postals with you very much," the sender, "Brownie," wrote from Perry, Oklahoma, on November 2, 1909. Brownie—Robert's sister, Marjorie—went on to inform Robert that she was going to a dance that night but lamented that it would have been nice to go with him. The card was addressed to "Mr. Robert Boles, Guthrie, Oklahoma." On

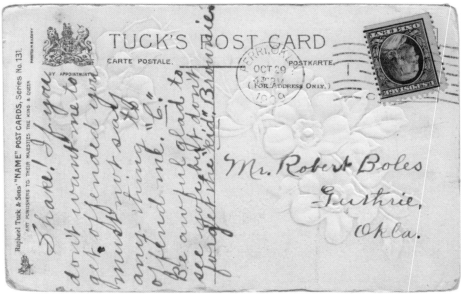

Front and back of postcard to Robert Boles from his sister Marjorie ("Brownie.")
The flowers are stamped reliefs. Mailed 1909.

Front and back of postcard to Robert Boles from "Edna B." "Coppered" lettering and border shimmer with a coppery ink. Mailed 1909.

October 29, 1909, Brownie sent a "Tuck's Post Card" from Raphael Tuck & Sons' "Name" postcard series that had Robert's name spelled out in flowery pink and gold script surrounded by roses. It contained carefully penned recriminations. "If you don't want me to get offended you must not say anything to offend me . . . Be awful glad to see you but don't forget the 'kid.' Brownie."

The only other card from 1909 that I came across had a coppery border and a colored-ink sketch of an Edwardian couple canoodling on a park bench. A police officer has his left hand up in a stop sign and his right hand brandishes a police baton in an attempt to put a halt to the amorous activity. The card is captioned with a rather forced attempt at a pun, "'Coppered' in the act." Postmarked October 21, 1909 from Perry, Oklahoma, the postcard was addressed to Robert in Guthrie with the message, "This is in answer to your card that I received May 25-09. Just found it. See?—Edna B." (I really wanted to know just what sort of postcard Great-grandfather Robert had sent to Edna B. in May of 1909 to prompt such a message in return.)

By 1910–11 Robert was receiving cards from all over the country, but most were from California and Oklahoma. (Or perhaps Robert was simply saving more cards in later years?) News of travels and moves, illnesses and fancy dances: The ins and outs of everyday life were refreshingly mundane to read. On December 22, 1910, for example, "Roy" sent Bob a note while Robert was in Williams, California: "From present indications it looks almost impossible for me to come up for Xmas. If I can get a sub to work for me, I will be up on the 6:55 Saturday night. However I wish you a Merry, Merry Christmas and a Happy New Year." (No word if Roy found a sub or not.)

The more of Robert's postcards I read, the more overwhelmed with minutiae I became. In many ways, it was like reading my great-grandfather's one-hundred-year-old text messages—if those messages had been handwritten on the back of a printed card, stamped, and mailed off to the recipient.

. . . .

Postcards trace their beginning to some seven decades earlier than Roy's note to Robert about coming up to visit for Christmas in 1910. There are a lot of ways to define the "first" postcard, but a generally agreed-upon earliest postcard dates to 1840, when the novelist and playwright Theodore Hook of London mailed himself a hand-colored picture card as a bit of a joke. The front of the card featured stuffy legal scribes clustered around a ridiculously large inkwell, scribbling away with equally ridiculous quill pens—an unflattering caricature straight out of a Dickens novel. Hook stuck a Penny Black stamp on the back of the image, addressed it to himself—Theodore Hook, Esq., Fulham—and had a laugh at the mockery he thought he was making of the postal service. (Hook's colleagues often noted his "wit and drollery.") The card sold for £31,750 in 2002 and contemporary British postal historian Edward Proud described the card's discovery as "[making] Hook the undisputed 'postal equivalent of the Earl of Sandwich,'" thus crediting Theodore Hook, Esq., of Fulham, with the invention of the postcard.[14]

However, Dr. Emanuel Herrmann of Vienna is far more commonly cited as the "inventor" of the postcard after an article he wrote for *Neue Freie Presse* proposed that the provision of a card with preprinted postage would be an advance in the efficiency of everyday correspondence. Why waste an entire letter and its postage, he argued, when just a few lines would do? Thus, on September 22, 1869, the Austrian Postal Department issued Post Office Regulation No. 21.18.916.1832 regarding the introduction of *Correspondenz-Karten* (correspondence cards) for domestic communication and declared that they were an acceptable category of mail. The Austrian Post Office promptly issued buff-colored cards that were imprinted with a yellow two-kreuzer stamp in the top right-hand corner. The card had three ruled lines on one side where the card was to be addressed to the recipient.[15] According to the official regulation, postcards that carried "offensive remarks" such as "obscenities, libelous remarks or other punishable acts" would not be delivered. *Correspondenz-Karten* went into circulation on October 1,

Korrespondenzkarten from Germany, without scenic landscapes,
simply for short correspondence, *c.* 1892. Printer unknown.

1869 and within the first three months, 2,926,102 cards were sold within Austria-Hungary.[16]

This success caught the attention of other European countries, and the government of the then North German Confederation was next to issue postcards, on July 1, 1870, with a price fixed at one silver groschen. (This was the same price as for an ordinary letter.) The first day *Korrespondenzkarten* went on sale in Germany, 45,468 cards were sold in Berlin alone. On March 1, 1872, the name was officially changed to *Postkarten*. The postcards had a picture on one side and space for a few lines of message. Postcards sold to tourists and locals alike, and their exponential popularity meant that Germany entered into an agreement with Austria-Hungary that postcards sent between the two nations would be delivered by the respective local mail services. Switzerland and the United Kingdom were next to formalize postcards as legitimate items of mail. Most of these cards were sent through domestic mail, as international carriers weren't sure what to make of the postage on postcards.

The question of how to send postcards internationally was solved a few years later in 1874 when 22 countries signed the Treaty of Bern. The treaty focused, in part, on how to legislate the delivery of mail between empires and was the first time that postcards were discussed on an international level. All participating countries agreed that it should be possible to send postcards internationally to members of the Universal Postal Union. (Postcards that were sent internationally before the treaty could be canceled by the postal systems as "Not Transmissible Abroad."[17]) "Today we give no thought when we send a postcard to a country overseas," historian Frank Staff points out; "such a common everyday action is assumed by many to have always been possible. Few people realize that it required days and hours of discussion at an international meeting attended by the top postal officials of the civilized countries of the world in order to come to an agreement to do this."[18] With the tricky issue of international postage and delivery ironed out, postcard sales increased even more.

Across Europe and the United States, picture postcards quickly became filled with all the different genres we've come to expect—political propaganda, tourism, and advertising, to name a few. Cards were issued in calls for world peace and incited anti-clerical feelings, and contained advertisements for charities and missionary efforts, quotes from famous literary figures, and picturesque scenes from various tourist destinations. In 1870 Prussia even issued "Field Post Cards" for their troops. The series offered "somewhat suggestive verses" and several cards that showed how military field post offices were being set up and run during training and armed conflicts.[19] (Historians and postcard collectors classify these "Field Post Cards" as the earliest propaganda postcards.) In the ensuing decades, a plethora of companies—from Curt Teich & Co. to Raphael Tuck & Sons, Ltd.—became synonymous with particular picture postcard genres, Americana, and mid-twentieth-century tourism.

Just about every country created and re-created the postcard in the mid- to late nineteenth century. Trade cards (advertisements) and "visiting cards" that depicted landscapes, monuments, and scenes across Europe were even earlier eighteenth-century predecessors to the global printed postcard industry. One early ancestor of postcards was the "mailed cards" that came with color-lithographed picture envelopes. On February 27, 1861, the U.S. Congress passed legislation that allowed such privately printed cards to be sent through the mail. This was the same year that stationer and printer John P. Charlton and Hymen Lipton in Philadelphia copyrighted what they called a "postcard."

By the 1870s the United States Post Office had taken to printing its own postcards, called "Pioneer Cards." For the ensuing three decades, the Post Office was the only U.S. institution allowed to print what could legally be called "post cards" for which postage was set at one cent. Private printers could continue to print and sell cards—as long as they called them something other than "post cards": commercial printers and stationers often offered "private mailing cards"—and these private cards were to be posted at the cost of two cents. It wasn't until May 19, 1898, that Congress passed the "Private Mailing Card Act" and the postage for postcards was uniformly set at one cent. This piqued public interest and the race was on to buy and send all manner of postcards. In the UK, the 1898 Imperial Penny Post Act meant that letters and postcards could be sent throughout the entire British Empire (and by 1905, the Penny Post Act included Australia and New Zealand) for a penny.[20]

By 1900 postcards began to look more like what we have come to expect them to look like. The divided format of the postcard, with lines for the address, appeared in the United States in 1907 (although many European countries had used the format for decades prior), and by 1915 most postcards had divided backs. A decade and a half later saw a trend for white borders and the rise of photographs being printed on postcard cardstock. The evolution of postcard styles offers a way to gauge the age and manufacture of historic postcards. But the plurality of postcard types demonstrates how flexible and adaptable the medium's technology was the world over.

The success of all these early cards, however, is owed to several social and technological components that all card makers had in common: relatively inexpensive postage available to the sender and the logistical means to deliver stamped cards to their recipients. In other words, the success of postcards depended on the technology to print images on cardstock and the existence of the social institutions that would charge postage and deliver letters.

. . . .

Theodore Hook, Esq., might technically have sent the earliest postcard but the ecosystem of making, sending, and receiving messages stretches back for millennia. Postcards—like those sent between Robert, "Brownie," and Edna B.—were part of a network of mass communication that itself was the result of a much, much older legacy of writing, sending, and receiving messages. To understand what postcards "do" or how they carry and deliver messages, we have to understand the social institutions that built them—postage, delivery routes, and the message's medium itself.

Front of Mount Shasta postcard to Robert Boles.
Pebbled texture and stamped photograph. Mailed 191?.

Verso of Mount Shasta postcard to Robert Boles.
The sender laments not having more room for her message. Mailed 191?.

"When did we decide that waiting for a response was worth our time? When did face-to-face exchanges cease to be sufficient for our needs?" media studies scholar Jason Farman asks in his 2018 book, *Delayed Response: The Art of Waiting from the Ancient to the Instant Worlds*. "When did we begin to develop technologies for sending messages to distant people in lands unknown? When did humans first start sending messages?"[21]

Finding the earliest examples of humans exchanging messages is difficult. Many of the materials that have been used to jot down messages throughout human history simply do not keep and will fade, crumble, or rot over time. Although archeologists have discovered paintings and artifacts from the Paleolithic and Stone Ages—from any number of sites across the globe—it is impossible to describe these various artifacts as "messages" in the same way that we talk about other person-to-person communiqués, as there is still so little known about the cultural cachet that Pleistocene-age artifacts carried within their various prehistoric cultures.

One of the oldest means of exchanging messages traces its origins back at least twelve thousand years to Australia, where Aboriginal peoples sent missives across vast distances with messengers carrying sticks. A message was dictated that was carved on these short, slender sticks with pictographs or with a pattern of various cuts that could be read by the recipient. Messages were delivered by foot and by boat; the majority of the sticks were used to convey specific details about gatherings or to honor someone. The mobile message sticks were not meant to live past their delivery; consequently it is impossible to estimate how many messages have been sent and received via stick in the thousands of years that they have been in use. Message sticks were, as Jason Farman notes, "typically single-use, single-event tools that didn't contain an 'archive' of knowledge . . . They were mankind's first 'mobile medium.'"[22] More significantly, today, message sticks are understood through the oral history passed down among Aboriginal peoples, who consider message sticks to be important in identity and culture.

Cuneiform clay tablet, Mesopotamia, *c.* 2052 BCE.

"There are a lot of different written means of communication where the sender doesn't necessarily expect a response," Farman noted as he and I spoke about postcards and the history of messages. "Letters, for example, were often sent not knowing if they would be received with the inherent uncertainty in postal delivery." But postcards, I pressed. What would it mean to send something without necessarily expecting a response? "Maybe the act of sending a postcard is more important than necessarily receiving it," Farman offered. "Sending the postcard is about representing yourself in a particular social and geographic space."[23]

In order to offer such a representation of self, however, one needs a way to ensure that the message will be reliably picked up and delivered.

Postal services are integral to the everyday maintenance of large, complex, sedentary societies. Put enough people in one place—or many densely populated places—and they'll need a way to send messages to each other. Postal systems—both government-run and private companies—are the means of building and maintaining communications throughout empires. They became a way to cope with the question of scale and how to effectively deliver more and more messages throughout history. From China to Europe to Persia to Chinggis Khan's empire across Central Asia, having a reliable way of sending and receiving messages is the infrastructure that empires are built on.

All organic, carbon-based media—parchment, papyrus, paper—will inevitably break down and decompose, but non-organic materials, such as fossilized bones, stone, and clay, preserve particularly well. Consequently, some of the earliest organized systems for sending and receiving messages are traced to the exchange of clay cuneiform tablets. It is possible that these "earliest" postal services simply reflect the preservation biases of materials in the historical and archeological records.

Archeologists can trace the exchange of clay tablet communiqués written in cuneiform to ancient Assyrian merchants somewhere around 1900 BCE. Clay cuneiform tablets show the minutiae of everyday life in ancient Babylonia, from business headaches to family heartbreaks. But because the cuneiform messages were written in clay, the ins and outs of everyday life in ancient Babylon are immortalized in ways that the missives' authors could hardly have imagined.

Letters from Mesopotamia: Official, Business, and Private Letters on Clay Tablets from Two Millennia is a compilation of transcribed and translated ancient cuneiform tablets originally published in 1967. Reading through translations of the cuneiform messages is refreshingly familiar to reading postcard messages. Translations of tablets described a landlord griping about a tenant. Moral outrage at being cheated in a business deal. Letters from significant others. A dense, impenetrable bureaucracy, where the decisions of a few elite courtiers and politicians deny petitioners' requests. Some messages were significant, some decidedly not. But because the tablets tended to be small—like postcards—the message was constrained by the medium.

For example, in one tablet from Babylonia around 1750 BCE, one Adad-abum has written to his father, Uzālum. In addition to apparently only trusting the messenger as far as he could throw him, Adad-abum petulantly reminds Uzālum to send the cloak that he has previously mentioned.

> Tell Uzālum: Your son Adad-abum sends the following message:
>   May the gods Šamaš and Wēr keep you forever in good health.
>
>   I have never before written to you for something precious I wanted. But if you want to be like a father to me, get me a fine string full of beads, to be worn around the head. Seal it with your seal and give it to the carrier of this tablet so that he can bring it to me. If you have none at hand, dig it out of the ground wherever (such objects) are (found) and send it to me. I want it very much; do not withhold it from me. In this I will see whether you love me as a real father does. Of course, establish its price for me, write it down, and send me the tablet. The young man who is coming to you must not see the string of beads. Seal it (in a package) and give it to him. He must not see the string, the one to be worn around the head, which you are sending. It should be full (of beads) and beautiful. If I see it and dislike(?) it, I shall send it back!
>   Also send the cloak, of which I spoke to you.[24]

This has a similar pattern of communication to what we might expect to find on a long-winded postcard. There's an expectation that the tablet is a means of reinforcing personal ties and that this particular message is part of a back-and-forth communication between the sender and the recipient—in this case between what we might assume is an exasperated father and a churlish son. Successful delivery of the tablet

Photo reproduction of *La Descente du Saint-Esprit* (The Right Hand of God Protecting the Faithful against the Demons) by Jean Fouquet, painted in the 15th century. Travel and the exchange of mail connected European cities during the Middle Ages and Renaissance.

requires that there is someone to physically carry the message from the sender ("the young man who is coming to you") across a geographic distance. Every element of social infrastructure necessary for postcards is present here, thousands of years before Theodore Hook, Esq., gets it in his head to mail the first postcard.

. . . .

Writing the message is one thing—being able to send and receive it is another. The Persian king Darius (521–486 BCE) is credited with the development of a formal postal system, which was created in order to pass along copies of his orders. This was—is—perhaps the most celebrated ancient postal system in the world. It grew to be a network for imperial orders as well as one that merchants and other ancient Assyrians were able to use for personal and commercial use. "It was the Persians who introduced the camel from Arabia into the Sahara to organize the postal service on this new desert road," historian Gerd Gropp notes. "Well known is the famous postal road through Anatolia to the royal residence in Susa."[25]

At the same time that Darius was establishing a formal system of sending and receiving messages, others were working to find ways to subvert it. The Greek ruler Histiaeus, for example, devised a means of transmitting sensitive messages away from the prying eyes of the Persian empire. According to the ancient Greek historian Herodotus, Histiaeus had a slave's head shaved and the message written on his scalp. He waited for the slave's hair to grow back, safely obscuring the message until the messenger's journey was complete. At his destination, the head would again be shorn and the message read.

Back in the world of cuneiform tablet communiqués, however, the speed at which they were delivered was the stuff of historical legend. "Nothing mortal travels so fast as these Persian messengers," declared Herodotus. "These men will not be hindered from accomplishing at their best speed the distance which they have to do, either by snow, or rain, or heat, or by the darkness of night. The first rider delivers his dispatch to the second, and the second passes it to the third and so it is borne from hand to hand along the whole line, like the light of the torch-race."[26]

Postal systems that facilitate sending and receiving messages are built out of three components: delivery routes, postage, and the type of material the message put in the mail is made from. In other words, in order for a message to be sent and received, it's necessary to have a route for that mail to travel along, and the postage pays for the labor of getting it from one place to another. Although people have sent each other messages throughout human history, the material that those messages have been written on has varied considerably throughout the centuries—which, unsurprisingly, has had an impact on how mail is sent and delivered.

After cuneiform tablets, messages were written on parchment, vellum, papyrus, paper, and a host of other mediums. Sprawling empires—from Rome to Greece, Egypt, China, Persia, and Mongolia—had postal systems integral to the everyday business of running a complex, bureaucratic empire. Sometimes these postal systems were public and available to anyone who could pay; sometimes they were simply an example of royal privilege and only used by the ruling elite. Incidentally, postal systems, much like the media and messages that they carry, have been invented and reinvented over the last five thousand years of human history, with each iteration reflecting cultural values and mores about who can receive messages, how they receive them, when, and why.

In Cicero's day, for example, mail was sent through a postal system that was maintained by Roman financiers, who had bought the right to collect taxes in the provinces from the Roman government. (Even Rome's provincial governors found this system to be the most reliable and effective for sending administrative missives back and forth.[27]) Two hundred years later, by the first century BCE, the imperial Roman post carried and delivered missives through the empire along a series of roads and ports, from Britain to Constantinople. By 100 CE journeys were marked by lodging places—mansions—located every 25 miles along roads, with relay stations—mutations—every 10 miles. Postal vehicles had two wheels and were drawn by two horses, as specified by Roman law.[28]

In Europe's Middle Ages, most postal routes followed older routes that had been developed during the Roman empire. During the twelfth century, for example, the Guild of Butchers in Germany established the so-called Butchers' Post, or *Metzger Post*, and members of the guild would carry letters with them while they traveled. This morphed into a formalized postal administration that lasted well into the 1500s and was eventually taken over by the postal system of the Holy Roman Empire. In 1160 the city of Barcelona established a mail system using a lay brotherhood that supplied mail services to the towns and villages in the area; they were required to wear a uniform and keep postal accounts. Almost three hundred years later, on July 20, 1444, postal authorities in

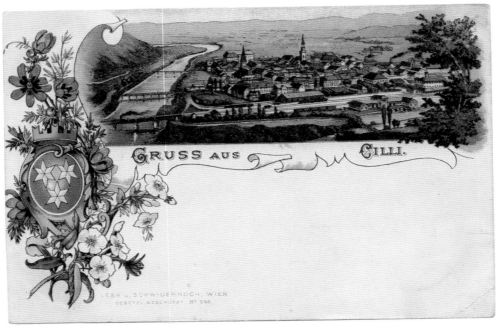

Postcard of Celje, Slovenia, c. 1892. Printer unknown. "Gruss aus Cilli" or "Greetings from Celje" offers a halcyon, uncomplicated view of the city.

Barcelona issued specific instructions to carriers: Bundles of letters were not to be untied, letters should only be delivered to the proper address, and special deliveries could be made at additional cost.

By 1200 a parallel postal system had emerged within Europe's universities, where messenger services exchanged messages between students and their families. Messengers working for the University of Paris would carry messages for students, but they would also carry and deliver mail for private paying individuals who wished for communications to be delivered elsewhere in Europe. In 1481 King Edward IV of England set up a "post system" to relay dispatches during a war with Scotland. Riders were stationed every 20 miles, and were therefore able to move a message upwards of 100 miles a day. Though King Edward's system was not public, today's British Royal Mail credits these routes as foundational in their history. (And it certainly wasn't just Europe that established postal routes. In 1402 the Ming emperor Yongle of China opened the Imperial Courier Service to those who wished to send private letters.) These postal systems became the basis for state-based postal systems, similar to the imperial ones used centuries before.[29]

As the plethora of smaller postal systems formalized and began delivering more and more mail, one of the constant issues was the tension between domestic and international deliveries. Postal delivery from the Butcher's Guild would only carry a letter so far. What if a merchant needed a letter sent to a supplier outside of its reach? As Europe began to ramp up its international trade and exploration, various European countries needed to find ways to carry messages greater distances.

In 1489 Johann von Taxis was named the first Imperial Postmaster of the Holy Roman Empire, with headquarters at Augsburg, and established a government-run postal system in Austria. And on January 18, 1505, Franz von Taxis signed an agreement with Spain to set up and operate a postal system for 12,000 livres a year. This system would exchange post between the present-day countries of Belgium and the Netherlands, the Court of Maximilian in Germany, and the courts of the kings of France and Spain, serving the cities of Paris, Lyons, Toledo, and Granada. This first international postal system was so successful that the aristocratic House of Thurn and Taxis (to which Johann and Franz belonged) served to meet Europe's postal needs until 1867, when the last remaining routes were sold to Prussia.[30]

Postal systems began to expand across large swaths of the world as European empires grew. Broadly, these different systems mapped themselves onto Europe's imperial expansions, their acquired European territories and, eventually, their colonies. As Darius, Cyrus, and the ancient Assyrians had found over a thousand years before, the administration of an empire is no small feat. Running it successfully requires that there is a way to move messages, orders, and information from the center—the capital or metropole—to the outskirts of the empire.

By the 1600s a plethora of different postal systems were in service across the globe. Some were owned and run by private companies and some were operated by governments. The delivery areas of many postal systems overlapped. Routes were set and maintained. (In fact, they could also be bought and sold.) New routes were constantly being developed. The more that were added and the more established they became, the more frequently messages were sent and delivered along them.

Not only were new postal routes emerging within and between empires, but these new routes often required multiple types of carriers to deliver the mail—everything from boats, to horses, to foot travelers. In 1668, for example, a mail service was established between Harwich, England, and Helvoetsluis, in the Netherlands, using English packet boats to deliver mail from Dover to Calais and vice versa. On this particular route, mail left London on Tuesdays and Fridays and left Helvoetsluis on Wednesdays and Saturdays, establishing a set route for mail as well as a predictable schedule of when it would be picked up and delivered. The route became so integral to the cultural fabric of the late seventeenth century that the service was not even interrupted during the Third Dutch War of 1692.

Establishing a set schedule for mail delivery was one of the most significant developments in post systems. Once regularly scheduled mail routes were established, the predictability that came with them became integral to sending and receiving messages via that postal system and would be for millennia to come—whether those messages arrived through cuneiform tablets, written letters, or printed postcards.[31]

. . . .

But postal systems are more than just delivery routes—they're also the infrastructures and labor to collect, sort, and deliver mail, and they have to do all of that within a budget that they themselves do not set. For centuries, various governments have found different ways to solve the question of how to ensure mail can be reliably sent and delivered, and by the time the United States Post Office Department was $17 million in the red in 1909, leveraging the global postcard obsession was simply a way to turn a deficit into a surplus.

What was it, though, about postcards, specifically, that made them so appealing? What did postcards offer people that cuneiform tablets, message sticks, parchment, and letters never did?

For one thing, postcards were the first means of communication that didn't depend on the sender or the receiver being of a particular socioeconomic class, as the cards were cheap and from early on included the requisite postage to ensure their delivery. "In the cafés and open-air restaurants and other places [in turn-of-the-twentieth-century Europe] it was common to see a postman with a mailing box strapped to his back, going from one table to the next, selling picture postcards and postage stamps," historian Frank Staff notes. "Then and there, people could write their messages and mail their postcards while the postman was waiting."[32] Postcards were also produced on a scale that no other form of communication had been before. They established personal connections and ties and did so over and over. From churches and missionary projects to newspaper advertisements to tourist locations, postcards could fill a plethora of communication niches that letters, envelopes, and tablets never could. It also didn't hurt that when they first came out, they were truly an oddity.

Postcard of Table Mountain, Cape Town, South Africa. Emphasizing
the Cape's iconic Table Mountain and clouds offers an idyllic landscape
of a country that was politically fraught at the beginning of the 20th century.
Printed by Raphael Tuck & Sons, c. 1900–1910.

Front of "real picture" —also called "real photo"—postcard from
La Huasteca near Monterrey, Mexico. Unmailed, c. 1910.

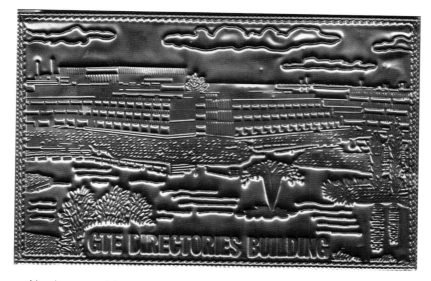

Novelty postcards have been popular for decades, and postcards have been made out of just about any material imaginable, including leather, wood, and botanical pressings. This "copper" postcard is a hammered sheet of copper wrapped around a traditionally printed postcard. The verso describes the postcard as a "Kopper Kard" and offers a two-sentence history of humankind's use of copper. Unmailed.

Like most communication technologies, what we call "postcards" developed independently in many places and in many times. And in each instance they were specifically fitted to particular cultural norms.[33] "When the archaeologists of the thirtieth century begin to excavate the ruins of London, they will fasten upon the picture postcard as the best guide to the spirit of the Edwardian era," Edwardian writer James Douglas facetiously put forward in 1907. "They will collect and collate thousands of these pieces of pasteboard and they will reconstruct our age from these strange hieroglyphs and pictures that time has spared."[34]

By the beginning of the twentieth century, from the United States to Canada, Great Britain, Europe, and parts of Asia and South America, postcards were being made, sold, and sent at a staggering rate. The global population hovered somewhere around 1.75 billion in 1920, but the number of postcards mailed around the world vastly outstripped the number of people in it. There isn't any other sort of material message communication or art form that has been so widely distributed among the world's population.

As such, postcards—even "old-timey" or historic ones—are so common that in 2004 Rudy Franchi, the collectibles appraiser for the U.S. television program *Antiques Roadshow*, suggested, "I would think that the item that we get the most of, on *Roadshow*, is postcards."[35] Franchi followed up his observation with what he called his "standard spiel" that most postcards, old though they may be, generally appraise anywhere from 25 cents to a dollar (although some are worth a great deal more.) Postcard collections, then, are about something—sentiment? nostalgia?—that is outside of financial valuation.

Postcards might have saved the United States Post Office from financial ruin in the early twentieth century, but their story is so much more than that of a stopgap measure in a massive governmental institution. Postcards were successful because they could draw on millennia-old social infrastructures like mail delivery routes and postage, and the fact that they were so lightweight and cheap. As such, they built the first worldwide social network.

TWO

THE MEANS OF MASS
PRODUCTION

....

My pen hovered over the blank message section.

I had found two old-fashioned Utah postcards for sale on eBay, and, on an impulse, I bought them to send to my grandmother and a niece who live in St. George and Provo. I thought that they would get a kick out of them. Now I was just trying to fill them out.

The fronts of the postcards were full of bright, vibrant colors. On one, green trees animated the walkway of Brigham Young University's campus and, on the other, "Greetings From Utah" was emblazoned in energetic orange, alternating block text and script surrounded by the state's iconic buildings and landscapes. Both postcards were printed on linen-like cardstock and if I held them under the light, I could see what looked like fibers running in a precise perpendicular weave. Each message and address side had a couple of lines explaining the postcard's front image as well as crediting Curt Teich & Co. with the color printing technology ("C. T. Art-Colortone") and the associated patent ("© Curt Teich & Co., Inc.") The blank message areas were a bit yellowed with age.

Looking up the postcards' serial numbers online through the Curt Teich Archives Collection at Newberry Library, I was able to pinpoint

Early wooden printing press, depicted in 1568 by Jost Amman.
These presses could produce up to 240 impressions per hour.

the postcards' printing dates to 1937 and 1941. Not only had these post-cards seen history, these postcards *were* history. Then I couldn't believe that I was actually considering sending my niece an 86-year-old artifact with something like "LOL, saw this and thought of you! Hope your semester's going well!" scribbled on the back.

What sort of historian was I, that I would take a decades-old post-card out of its plastic collecting sleeve, slap a stamp on it, and stick it in the mail? It wasn't the cost (they were something like $2.99 apiece), it was the principle. These postcards had survived for decades and here I was getting ready to subject them to the tender ministrations of the United States Postal Service.

So I hesitated.

. . . .

It wasn't as if I couldn't buy these historic Curt Teich & Co. postcards again—the internet is full of them in various conditions. Some of the postcards for sale are blank, some are not. Scroll through enough eBay and Etsy listings and you will conclude that Curt Teich & Co. postcards are nothing if not abundant. In fact, historian Jeffrey Meikle estimates that the Curt Teich & Co. factory in Chicago produced something like a billion postcards over six decades in the twentieth century. And Curt Teich & Co. was not the only company printing postcards on this scale. (Raphael Tuck & Sons, the Detroit Publishing Company, and the Alfred Holzman Co., for example, were popular printers, to say nothing of a plethora of other printers around Europe and the rest of the world.) Historians estimate that during the first decade and a half of the twentieth century, sixty postcard factories in Germany alone employed more than 12,000 workers, with another 30,000 in France. All of these factories across the globe made sure that postcards could be printed and reprinted en masse.

"Greetings from Utah." Curt Teich & Co. postcard, 1937. The back caption tells us, "Nature was in a lavish mood when she ladled out a dozen National Parks and National Monuments to Utah." Purchased and mailed by author in 2019.

Because postcards were mass-produced, they've occupied a unique niche in how art and material culture intersect. Postcards are copies—art and images that are reproduced over and over. (And early postcards didn't even have images; they were just physical spaces on which to move short messages.) When imagery was added to postcards, they were, critics would sniff, invariably kitsch. But postcards had an unmistakable appeal.

"The whole province of genuineness is beyond technological . . . reproducibility," philosopher and cultural critic Water Benjamin argues in *The Work of Art in the Age of Mechanical Reproduction*. "In making many copies of the reproduction, it substitutes for its unique incidence a multiplicity of incidences. And in allowing the reproduction to come closer to whatever situation the person apprehending it is in, it actualizes what is reproduced."[1] In other words, a reproduction—in this case, a postcard—might not be a singular work of art; nevertheless, a postcard carries the ability to invoke a feeling or "aura" in its audiences. And this ability is no small part of postcards' popularity.

"The massive proliferation of copies did away with authenticity insofar as it was a link to an originating, or founding, object," writer Celeste Olalquiaga observes in *The Artificial Kingdom: A Treasury of the Kitsch Experience*. "Mass reproduction contradictorily helped to reassert the one-of-a-kind quality of objects usually associated with authenticity and conceptually represented in the 'aura' . . . that surrounds certain experiences and things."[2]

But postcards didn't have to be singular and individually unique to be popular and functional art, kitschy though they often were. Unlike lithographic facsimiles or reproductions, postcards don't even beg the question of where the original ends and the copy begins. Postcards are simply the art of copies—but each postcard, each copy, has a singular history. And with the media so financially and easily accessible across socio-economic lines, postcards worked to bring people reliable, inexpensive communication.

Postcards grew out of the modernization and mechanization of production across the United States and Europe in the mid-nineteenth century; their history is inexorably a product of industry, technology, and capitalism. Postcards were the perfect twentieth-century icons of mass consumerism and production, with the ink, paper, and presses to prove it.

. . . .

The mass production of postcards begins centuries before the Curt Teich & Co. postcards I found on eBay were printed—it starts with Johannes Gutenberg. When Gutenberg invented a mechanical, moveable type printing press, it fundamentally transformed the way in which information traveled. Gutenberg's moveable type meant that text could be assembled, printed, disassembled, and the information disseminated faster than any one-off, hand-scribed documents, codices, and manuscripts of earlier centuries. The introduction of this sort of printing technology ensured that text could and would be introduced to readers on a scale that was unprecedented in the history of putting ink to paper.[3]

Gutenberg wasn't the first person to put together the idea—or even the machinery—of a printing press. Prior to Gutenberg's invention, European printing, like its earlier Chinese counterpart, used carved wooden blocks to be able to reproduce pages with identical text. And Gutenberg wasn't even the first to use moveable or metal type. Between 1041 and 1049, for example, Pi Shêng of China developed a moveable clay type. Korean printing presses utilized a metal type a century or two before Gutenberg's and around fifty years before printing came to Europe.[4]

Thus the success of Gutenberg's printing press isn't just the story of an apparatus that could easily move letters around. It is also a story about ink. ("It should . . . be remembered that the discovery of an oil-based printing ink by Gutenberg was just as important as his development of the use of moveable metal type and the press," historian Colin Bloy argues in *A History of Printing Ink*.[5]) Earlier printing ink used for wooden block copying was a thin, water-based fluid that was more or less identical to the ink used for scribing by hand. For example, a recipe for black ink from China dating to 251 CE had the creator mix lampblack—pigment made from soot—in a mortar and gum solution until it was like a paste. The solution was placed into molds to dry and then sold in sticks of ink pigment and binding agent. Printers "hydrated" the pigment base on a concave stone and added water so they could apply the ink to wooden blocks; the viscosity and thickness of the ink could be controlled through the amount of water added to each batch. (Archeologists trace the earliest use of ink sticks to China's Neolithic period, over 10,000 years ago.) Water-based inks were well suited for parchment, vellum, and printing with wooden blocks, but those sorts of inks just oozed off of the metal of Gutenberg's moveable typeface. It was impossible to keep the metal type inked and for that ink to not look "globby" on the paper it was printed on.

Metal type presses like Gutenberg's would require an ink with a different base to give the liquid a viscous, thick consistency that would stick to the typeface. Gutenberg developed an oil-based alternative using oils similar to those used by contemporary painters, giving the ink more in common with a varnish or a paint than with the water-based inks used by scribes. This oil-based ink showed Gutenberg's familiarity with oil varnishes that were used in conjunction with turpentine, amber, and sandarac—resin from a small, cypress-like tree from northern Africa. "Just as master painters made their own colours, Gutenberg was his own ink maker," historian Ted Bishop notes in his book *The Social Life of Ink*.[6]

The smooth, even black ink associated with Gutenberg's Bibles contains carbon, with small reflective grains of graphite, as well as high levels of copper, lead, titanium, and sulfur, giving the ink a reflective sheen as well as an intense, even color. The paint was transformed into ink suitable for the printing press. In addition to its thick viscosity, oil-based ink dried rather uniformly and quickly.

In some early printed Bibles, Gutenberg experimented with the idea of printing with more than one color and using red for the beginning and ending of certain verses. Ultimately, however, multi-colored (polychrome) printing was abandoned in favor of the efficiency that printing in just black afforded. But the use of multiple colors in printing did become a show of technological prowess in printing in the ensuing centuries, although printing texts with multiple colors would always prove difficult.[7] ("In the field of colour, ink-making has come a long way recently, largely due to the efforts of the pigment makers, but the colours of today are brighter and more usable than ever before," Colin Bloy noted as recently as 1967, underscoring the point that ink technology is in constant flux. "The ink-maker can concentrate more colour into an ink, which means thinner films can be used. Fluorescent colours have arrived since the war [Second World War], and recent work on fluoride chemistry promises us even more startling colours in the not-too-distant future. Metal pigments are no longer the problem they used to be."[8]) In other words, as color technology and chemistry unfolded, the spectrum of colors available for printing inks increased, as did the efficacy of those new inks actually adhering to their intended surfaces.

In addition to ink and moveable type, Gutenberg's printing also introduced the question of what paper to print on. For something like two millennia, parchment—writing media made from specially prepared animal skins—had dominated how people wrote documents, manuscripts, and books. If something was to be permanent, the logic went, then it should be written down, and on parchment. "Parchment was for handwritten documents and manuscripts, and printing was to be done exclusively on paper, which considerably increased the demand for it," journalist Mark Kurlansky notes in *Paper: Paging through History*. "But paper was no longer regarded as a low-quality material to be used only for inconsequential jottings."[9] This is where paper begins to transition to a different place in the history of European printing.

At its most basic, paper is a made of broken-down cellulose fibers that are mixed with water and diluted. Throughout history, paper's cellulose fibers have come from wood, bark, and grasses as well as cotton, silk, and even seaweed. (Cellulose, $C_6H_{10}O_5$ in chemical parlance, was "discovered" by French chemist Anselme Payen in 1838, but had been known in a practical sense for millennia.) The liquid solution of cellulose and water is ladled out onto a screen to drain, leaving a very thin layer behind. This is paper.

Popular history has credited the invention of paper to a eunuch in the Han court named Cai Lun in 105 CE; archeological discoveries of ancient paper in Central Asia push the date of paper back even earlier. In other words, from its very invention, paper has been a technology that requires constant tinkering to meet the demands of its ink as well as the ideas and intent behind it. In 1455, Gutenberg completed printing approximately 180 copies of the Bible—a success that showcased the interdependence of art, technology, craft, industry, and science. A Gutenberg Bible has 1,286 pages and 2,500 pieces of type, and cost 30 guilders per copy, available only via the fifteenth-century equivalent of a preorder. Each Bible weighs close to 14 lb. "Printing gave paper standing," Kurlansky clarifies, "it too was enduring and important, a sentiment that has itself endured."[10]

Thus what we call "print" is really hundreds of decisions about paper, ink, and how to combine them. From a historical perspective, "print" is about choosing handwritten script in earlier medieval centuries or opting for text produced with a press in the post-Gutenberg eras. Print is how a message is communicated and the material thing that connects an author with an audience—the sender with the receiver. Moreover, print is a social process and leaves its mark on the material world in both its end product—the thing that's printed—and the material culture that's necessary to create it.

"Media has always been social," historian Marissa Nicosia explained to me. "Early modern technologies of print were designed to connect people with ideas, and each other—these technologies were remarkably successful at achieving this goal. Print moved through established social networks and allowed those networks to expand."[11]

In the post-Gutenberg centuries, print—with its presses and types, paper and documents, inks and alchemy—ensured that media could be replicated over and over. For 150 years, postcards took advantage of this, but they were certainly not the first medium to do so.

. . . .

Once the Gutenberg press made mass printing feasible, people were faced with the question of what to print. Bibles, of course. Books, naturally. Gutenberg even interrupted the print runs of the iconic Bibles to print religious indulgences, which proved to be much more lucrative. But entire genres of literature sprang up around the possibility of creating cheap, practically disposable printed materials. From ballads and broadsides to pamphlets and playbills, the circulation of ephemeral printed materials changed people's relationship with how they consumed—how they read—media. Centuries later, postcards would prove to be no different.

Cheap, disposable print can be found all over the world. By the latter half of the sixteenth century, the shelf-life of any printed matter that wasn't a "proper" book was expected to be short. This sort of cheap communication was to be printed, purchased, and then discarded. This offers the best historical precursor to how postcards would be printed, consumed, and circulated some three hundred years later.

"Any study of the impact of printing in England must take account of the fact that one of the first widespread and widely affordable forms of the printed word was the song," historian Tessa Watt argues. Printed ballads worked their way through all sorts of social strata, from alehouses to markets to being sung by minstrels in the households of the nobility and gentry. "Thousands of ballads were churned from the London printing presses, not only to be read, but to be sung to popular tunes."[12]

In the second half of the sixteenth century there were roughly 3,000 distinct ballads published in England. Watt estimates that if two hundred copies was the smallest print run that a printer would consider setting type for, that would mean there was an absolute minimum of 600,000 printed copies of ballads in circulation. If print runs were larger, between 1,000 and 1,250 copies, as was typical for books of the time, the number of copies would be something like 3–4 million. And those estimates presume that there was only one print run of each ballad—for popular songs, it's safe to assume that there would have been multiple printings.[13]

Single-page broadsides—printed pages that served as proclamations, the early modern equivalent to contemporary news feeds or advertisements—became quite popular alongside their ballad counterparts. The cost of most broadsides was only a penny and many were priced anywhere from a third to half a penny. "For a peny you may have all the Newes in England, of Murders, Flouds, Witches, Fires, Tempests, and what not, in one of the Martin Parkers Ballads," English writer Henry Peacham described in his 1641 treatise *The Worth of a Penny*.[14] But what is most significant is that they were never meant to last. While books were collected, curated, and carried a certain amount of cultural cachet and seriousness, cheap print was meant to be read but not saved.

But cheap print was also made to be circulated, and it was produced and dispersed on a massive scale. "The distribution of cheap print relied especially on a network of wayfarers: minstrels, broadside ballad sellers, interlude players, petty chapmen," Watt explains.[15] Historian Margaret Spufford has carefully mapped out where chapmen (those who sold cheap print, namely chapbooks) were licensed in England and Wales in 1697–8. London, for example, had over five hundred licensed chapmen and the densities of selling licenses followed the trade and mail routes, emphasizing that it's not enough for the paper to be printed—it needs to end up in the hands of readers.[16] This pattern—how cheap print could be efficiently distributed—would hold up centuries later when postcard agents and distributors were the means through which towns could commission postcards from large companies, or stores could obtain postcards for their customers.[17] ("Scarce a town in America but has its postcard views and its postcard dealers," the *Times-Democrat* newspaper of New Orleans noted on January 2, 1909.[18])

Not only was cheap, disposable print in greater circulation by the end of the sixteenth century, but all that print required a plethora of institutions and social networks to move it. In the centuries after Gutenberg, cheap print became ubiquitous across Europe and was bought, read, and moved across social strata.[19] And how people read, used, circulated, and disposed of cheap print inevitably set the stage for how postcards would find their cultural niche hundreds of years later.

. . . .

A plethora of postcard companies around the world popped up at the turn of the twentieth century to meet the insatiable demand for printed picture cards. American manufacturer Curt Teich & Co. became one of the most dominant and iconic postcard industries of the midtwentieth century. Ask someone to describe an archetypal postcard and the odds are good that what they will pick—whether they know the name of the company or not—would be something like the postcards Curt Teich & Co. produced.

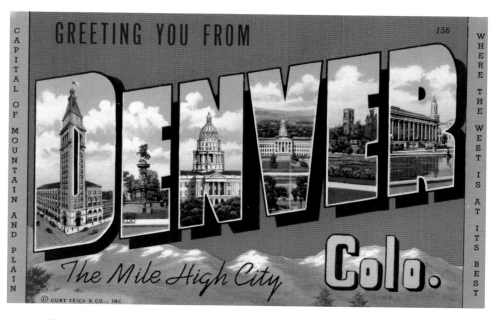

"Greeting You from Denver, Colo. The Mile High City." Printed by Curt Teich & Co., 1941.

"The miniature images of linen view cards . . . portrayed the American scene as shimmering with promise during the uncertain times of the Great Depression and World War II," historian Jeffrey Meikle summarizes in *Postcard America: Curt Teich and the Imaging of a Nation*. "Their saturated colors provided a popular view of the United States not displayed in grainy newspaper photos, high-contrast *Life* magazine photos, or the stark documentary work of photographers such as Dorothea Lange and Walker Evans."[20]

Made and shipped from Chicago, Curt Teich & Co. postcards offered a coherent, collective Americana aesthetic thanks to the company's innovative printing methods and its easily recognizable linen-looking cardstock. (History and postcard literature often refer to these as "linen postcards.") From 1931 through the early 1950s, Curt Teich & Co. published about 45,000 different postcards with specific, singular views of the United States that ranged from natural landscapes to sweeping cityscapes. Curt Teich & Co. postcards seemed to offer an artistic unity —real or not—to the United States that bridged both geography and social strata.

The story of Curt Teich postcards starts, unsurprisingly, with Curt Otto Teich, who emigrated to the United States from Germany, arriving in Chicago in 1895. His grandfather, Friedrich Teich, was a local official and poet who operated a print shop and published a newspaper in Lobenstein, a picturesque town in what is today central Germany, close to the border of Poland. From the late 1890s to the 1910s, the print shop of the extended Teich family produced postcards in their hometown. The postcard style had flowing, cursive script—"Gruss aus Lobenstein" ("Greetings from Lobenstein")—and tended toward cutesy, halcyon pastoral scenes and the occasional building or iconic bit of the town's architecture. These were similar in manufacture (using lithographic printing technology) to the hundreds of millions of other late nineteenth-century postcards that were unendingly popular across the world, particularly in Europe, Russia, and the United States, but unique in the artistic genre.[21]

When Curt Teich arrived in Chicago, he found work as a printer and, thanks to a loan from his brother Max, began to establish a viable printing business there that worked with newspapers and magazines. In the early days of Curt Teich & Co., the company functioned more as a purveyor of postcards from Germany, importing postcards and then reselling them in the United States. Manufacture came later; but as a printer, Teich was perfectly poised to explore the nascent market of color lithograph souvenir postcards that began to emerge in the United States, as enthusiasm for the missives began to build up steam.

By 1904 Teich had begun to experiment with printing his own postcards in the United States, using a traditional lithographic printing technique. Such printing used smooth, flatbed plates made of limestone or metal, with an image or text etched onto the plate and then transferred to paper using oil-based inks. More specifically, the image or text was drawn onto the plate using a fat-based medium (like a wax crayon) that ensured that the plate could hold up to multiple applications of water and acids. A weakly acidic solution of gum arabic was applied to the plate, and created a layer that would not stick to oil-based paints. When a lithographic plate was moistened, the etched parts of the stone—with the text or image—retained the water on the "positive side" of the image.

When printers rolled ink over the stones, the water-and-gum-saturated areas repelled it. The ink would adhere only to the hydrophobic parts of the plate and could be transferred to a blank page of paper. (Incidentally, the invention of lithographic printing in 1796 was originally targeted toward printing cheap theatrical works and then being able to put those works into circulation quickly without a costly investment.) Not only could it be transferred to paper, but it could be done so hundreds of times. Lithographic printing with multiple colors—formally known as polychrome or chromolithography—was incredibly popular in the mid-nineteenth century and was used to print everything from military maps to cabaret advertisements. Most nineteenth-century postcard manufacturers used lithographic printing of some sort to print the same image over and over.

Like Gutenberg's moveable type printing press, early lithographic printing technology depended on understanding the chemistry of printing ink and how to create multiple copies of the same thing. And lithography quickly grew to successfully print images in multiple colors—a feat that earlier printing presses struggled with. Although attempts at lithographic printing in multiple colors came quickly after the development of the technique, printers were able to successfully move beyond monochrome printing by 1837. But the complexity of multiple colors meant a compounding complexity in printing apparatuses—each color had its own lithographic stone, and each time a different color was added, the paper went through the printer again, with that color and stone adding another step in the overall printing process.

"Traditional lithography had employed horizontal flatbed presses that printed no more than 250 sheets per hour even when mechanized," Meikle points out. This had serious implications for printing postcards. "And lithographic stones wore out so quickly that the Detroit Publishing Company [then a rival to Curt Teich & Co.], which typically used nine or ten stones and occasionally as many as fifteen for the velvety colors of its secret process, was continually preparing new editions of its better-selling cards."[22]

By the time Curt Teich & Co. was working to expand both the quantity and quality of their printed postcards, the company found that they were running up against technical obstacles of image clarity and ink chemistry. The company attempted a halftone style of printing and these prints were of such poor print quality that the postcards did not sell well, especially when compared with the incredibly high-quality postcards that Curt Teich & Co. had imported from Germany in the previous years. (Halftone printing is a technique that relies on variously sized dots of ink to provide the illusion of solid color coverage. It reduces the amount of ink required per print, but it can reduce the clarity of an image's detail.) In fact, the first cards sold so poorly that Curt Teich & Co. was $75,000 in debt in 1907, equivalent to $2 million today.

Offset press operator at Curt Teich & Co. factory, 1910.

Curt Teich & Co. factory employees working a fleet of press machines, c. 1910s.

Two years later, however, Curt Teich managed to push the company to profitability thanks to the then-new Payne-Aldrich Tariff that meant Curt Teich & Co. could undercut German postcard sellers who had exported very cheap postcards to the United States for decades. (Recall that this was the point at which the United States Post Office was in a financial crisis and looking to postcards to bail it out.) In addition to the boost from the new tariff, the company also managed to hit on an innovative printing method, known as offset lithography, that ensured higher-quality color printing of the landscapes and scenes featured on the postcards.[23]

The switch to offset lithographic printing marked a distinct change in how Curt Teich & Co. put ink to paper—or, rather, image to postcard. The high-speed rotary press used zinc plates—not the traditional ones made of limestone—and three long, cylindrical rollers that would carry sheets of paper through the press. Traditional lithographic printing applied ink directly onto the plate and then put the paper to plate. Offset lithography applied ink to the plate and transferred the ink to a rubber surface (a roller, in the case of postcards) before the paper was run through the rubber rollers for printing. The additional, intermediary step of the rubber surface is what made the technique "offset." The technique meant that a rotary press could print postcards on paper sheets at a greater speed and at a higher print quality than before, and the result was a cleaner, crisper image.[24] Offset lithography also took advantage of bright, new inks that were coming onto the print market and the process used less ink overall. It was popular for magazines, newspapers, and, of course, postcards.

In 1909 Curt Teich & Co. was poised to produce the postcards Americans clearly wanted to send, and to print those postcards on a massive scale. But even with Teich's new printing equipment, which he had imported from Germany, he found that the presses he needed to produce the postcards simply weren't available. So Teich commissioned Walter Scott Company of Elizabeth, New Jersey, to build a press that would be able to print sheets of paper that measured 38 by 52 inches. The company continued to refine the printing process itself. By the time Curt Teich & Co. undertook its first mass order in 1910, they had hit on a successful process for mass-printing high-quality postcards. (In addition to experimenting with various print technologies, the company employed artists to paint various media. For example, on September 11, 1906, the company placed an advertisement in the *Chicago Tribune* looking for "Young Ladies to Paint Leather Cards."[25])

All Curt Teich & Co. postcards started as photographs. Transferring the images from photograph to postcard took a plethora of employees and person-hours. Once a postcard was commissioned by a city or company, the work order would enter Curt Teich & Co. in the composing and retouching department, which was responsible for contributing the text on the front and the captions on the back of the postcard. Then the image would go to the retouch artists who, using the original photo as a reference, would use an airbrush—supplemented with a fine-pointed brush of sable hair—to paint directly onto a copy print of the photo. The artists pasted a translucent layer of rubber cement over their now-painted photograph. Areas of the image were blocked off with tissue paper and the image was airbrushed with different hues, thus boosting the color block contrast in the images. (In 1910 Curt Teich & Co. was advertising as far away as New York City and St. Louis to recruit artists for "Litho for stipple and crayon work" that offered a "steady position" in the company.[26]) Colors were made more vibrant by simply applying more paint. Edges, lines, and details were then sharpened by artists.

All of that, however, simply got the Curt Teich & Co. factory to their "original" image that they could then run through the lithographic and later offset lithographic process—chromolithographic, because multiple colors were involved.[27] Some postcard sales agents, like G. I. Pitchford, who worked in the American Southwest, also found huge success in taking the initial photographs for postcards, as the agents "had plenty of opportunities to pull over to the side of the road and snap a photo of a vista, building, or scene he thought—nay, knew—would

DIAL No. 6A-H771	ORDER NO. K 60622 DATE 5-11-1936	DEPT.	DATE COMPLETED

RETOUCHING
ENGRAVING
PHOTO LITHO
COMPOSING
LITHO ART

Photos for this Customer

CUSTOMER NELSON TAVERN,
LEBANON, MO.

STYLE PHOTO COLORIT, WHITE BORDER

(All of this on address side)

6 M FC	SIZE 3½ x 5½

PLACE OF TITLE: Upper, Lower, Center—Border — Follow Layout
Title in Plate   Yes   No   Copyright in Plate   Yes   No
Title in full

FRONT N.   R. M.   Yes   No
R. M. to cover part of Mess. Space, entire Mess. Space, entire Front
Trade Mark   Yes   No   Special type as sample
IMPRINT: Customer   C. T. Imprint   No Imprint

RETOUCHING DEPARTMENT
Submit — Sketch — Layout — Retouched Photo — Wash Drawing
Follow Layout

PHOTO LITHO
Rephoto   NEG. NO.

_____Photograph each - Size 5x7 - 8x10 - 10x12
_____Prints each from_____ Negatives MATTE or GLOSSY
Mount on CARD, CLOTH, with hinge - or without hinge - Not mounted
See Salesman, Customer, or Sample for Position, Office
DELIVER   Straighten Photo
Negative — Line — Halftone — Combination.
Dry — Wet — Pancromatic — Color Separation.
Transfer — Paper Process — New Process.
Stripping — White Border — Full Face.
Blue Print — Handcolor — Black & White Proof.   Titles—Red, Blue.

Screen { 120 / 133 / 150 / 175 }

COLOR DESCRIPTION

THIS IS THE SAME COTTAGE AS SHOWN IN 6A-H772. LAMP POST IS BLACK WALNUT, AMBER GLASS SHADE.
COTTAGE ON RIGH DIFFERENT KINDS OF STONES, SEE COLORED PICTURE.

CUSTOMER | PHOTO PROPERTY OF C. T. & CO. | RETURN PHOTO   YES   NO

PHOTO RETURNED TO | PHOTO USED FOR

Curt Teich & Co. was in correspondence with postcard commissioners—
in this case with a guest house along U.S. Route 66 in Lebanon, Missouri.
Production file for final postcard, 1936.

All Curt Teich & Co. postcards started as photographs. The initial photographs
were processed by artists at Curt Teich & Co. to create their iconic postcard style.
When the postcard was finalized, it was straightforward to print as many copies as
were desired in various print runs. Production file for final postcard, 1936.

GUEST HOUSE No. 3

NELSON DREAM VILLAGE — U.S. HIGHWAY No. 66 AND No. 5 — LEBANON, MO.

make a profitable postcard," journalist Ben Marks explained.[28] "It was Pitchford's job to sell postcards, a task he was, by all accounts, extraordinarily good at," Marks describes in *Collector's Weekly*. "For him, though, source photos, accompanied by detailed instructions for the retouchers, were an essential component of his success."[29] Photographs submitted by cities and towns were "often stupefyingly dull upon arrival" but the artists at Curt Teich & Co. made America all the most interesting, one postcard at a time.[30]

In 1911 Curt Teich & Co. built a three-story brick plant in the far north side of Chicago in what was then the new industrial district. By 1912, Curt Teich & Co. were able to supply Woolworth's with postcards that were sold at ten cents for a dozen—what would eventually be millions of postcards. Within a few short years, Curt Teich & Co. had so effectively cornered the market of mass production that it was able to help put other American postcard manufacturers out of business. (For example, in 1913 fifteen American postcard printers went out of business and by 1914 the National Association of Post Card Manufacturers had canceled its annual meeting.[31]) By 1922 the plant simply couldn't accommodate the growing company, and Curt Teich & Co. expanded to a five-story brick factory. The manufacturing plant (no longer just a mere print shop) extended eastward to the next street. The new establishment offered an industrial workflow with dedicated floors to art and photography, including pressrooms with thirty printing presses on the first two floors.[32]

However, the intricacies of changes in color process and paper are myriad, full of hundreds of decisions about how to fine-tune the process of putting ink to cardstock; each step of development is the result of experimentation and tinkering. Just because Curt Teich & Co. hit on offset lithographic printing with oil-based inks early on in their business didn't mean that the company stopped experimenting with new inks, papers, and printing technologies. There was a push in the late 1920s, for example, to see if it was possible to use water-soluble inks inspired by the French printer Jean Berté; these inks were thinner and boasted

"The Post Card Man: I Have the Winning Cards," 1932. This Curt Teich & Co.
postcard features one of the company's longtime photographers and reps,
B. P. Atkinson of New Hampshire.

colors that were richer and more striking than what was possible using lithographic inks. Water-based inks, however, have difficulty sticking to metal typesettings—the reason why Gutenberg's oil-based inks were so historically significant. In order for water-soluble inks to stick to postcards, especially on the scale of Curt Teich & Co. production, something would have to change in the printing process, and that something was the texture of the cardstock paper Curt Teich & Co. used. "Several factors—economic, technical, and aesthetic—joined in a transformation that rendered obsolete the halftone-lithographic cards of the previous twenty years, with their sharp photographic outlines and delicate blue and pink washes," Meikle notes.[33]

When the newly developed brilliant water-based ink colors were printed on the flat cardstock from the 1910s and 1920s, the ink would absorb into the card and become dull and faded over time. To provide more surface area to the cardstock, Teich experimented with an embossing roller that would leave a textured surface, thus facilitating faster drying. (And if the ink dried faster, it couldn't run, bleed, and eventually

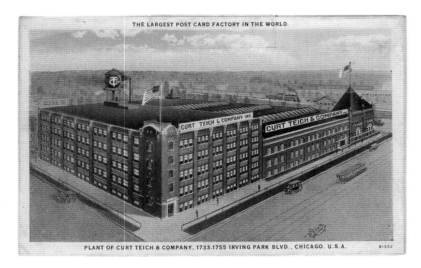

THE LARGEST POST CARD FACTORY IN THE WORLD.

CURT TEICH & COMPANY INC

CURT TEICH & COMPANY

PLANT OF CURT TEICH & COMPANY, 1733-1755 IRVING PARK BLVD., CHICAGO, U.S.A.

Postcard of Curt Teich & Co. postcard factory. Printed c. 1901–8.

fade over time.) The textured surface looked quite a bit like linen and thus "linen postcards" became de rigueur for printers looking to exploit new, brilliant colors. Not only was the new cardstock innovation a way to use new colors, but the changes in ink and printing technology meant that less ink was used per postcard, thus dropping the manufacturing costs for Curt Teich & Co. even further.[34] Despite the ever-experimental nature of his postcard technologies, Teich remained staunch in the conviction that the cost to consumers for these linen-like, brightly colored cards could not run to more than a penny a postcard.

The bumpy peak-and-valley texture of inked postcards became synonymous with Curt Teich & Co. postcards but also with other printers looking to imitate their popularity. Ironically, there were no Curt Teich postcards in my extended family's postcard collection, despite their being so iconic. (I would like to think that Great-grandmother Mary Virginia Stuart was savvy and fashionably chic enough to be sending Curt Teich & Co. postcards—and that it was her correspondents who were unable to latch onto the Curt Teich & Co. postcard fad, so I wouldn't have them in the collection of her received postcards.) But the postcards that I did find, from all over the United States, reflected the changes in postcard technology and manufacture.

I could definitely see that shift in printing technologies in the shoe-box of postcards that I looked through. By the time I got to postcards from the 1930s and '40s, the lithographic prints from 1910s and '20s postcards looked particularly faded and pink-washed. Understanding the differences in printing technology is, of course, how postcard collectors and connoisseurs are able to date historic postcards. Being able to parse out how a postcard entered circulation—and ended up in a family collection, an institution's archive, or simply relegated to history's dustbin—is a different sort of detective work altogether.

The demand for mass production of postcards, however, did not escape the watchful eyes of early postcard critics. They were more than just kitsch "art"; critics saw them as kitsch communication. In 1906 John Walker Harrington took his readers to task in a satirical article for *American Illustrated Magazine* where he calls postcards "epistolary sloth," in no small part because the origin and manufacture of early twentieth-century postcards could be traced to non-American compa-nies. Indeed, Harrington's criticisms read as a combination of literary snobbery and not-so-thinly-veiled nationalism; he coined the term "postal carditis" to describe the symptoms of millions of people falling victim to the billions of available postcards and the moral degradation that was surely to follow this mass-produced medium.

"Postal carditis and allied collecting manias are working havoc among the inhabitants of the United States," Harrington sneered. "The germs of these maladies, brought to this country in the baggage of tourists and immigrants, escaped quarantine regulations, and were propagated with amazing rapidity." Apparently, simply insinuating a connection between the cheap, printed medium of postcards and the immigrants coming through Ellis Island wasn't sufficient to make his point, and Harrington winds up for his punchline. "Unless such manifestations are checked, millions of persons of now normal lives and irreproachable habits will become victims of faddy degeneration of the brain."[35] It would appear that Harrington had very conveniently forgotten that printers and stationers in Philadelphia and across the United States had been busy printing out postcards for decades. And it is impossible not to wonder just what Harrington would have made of postcards bringing the United States Postal Service into the black over the next five years.

The point about print that emerges from the Curt Teich & Co. story is that it's not enough to simply print a lot of postcards—to truly dominate the postcard market, postcards had to be printed on a gargantuan scale. Plenty of other companies were either importing printed postcards from places like Germany or printing postcards themselves, but Curt Teich & Co. was able effectively to undercut them. And once Curt Teich & Co. postcards comfortably settled into being America's go-to purveyor of postcards, it filled that role for the next several decades, even as the demand for postcards dropped across America.

After Teich's death in 1974, the company was sold to Regensteiner Publishers (who continued to print at the Chicago factory until 1978); in 1978 the rights to the company name and its patented processes were sold to the Irish firm John Hinde Ltd.[36] In 1990 the factory was converted to Postcard Place Lofts, with the letters C & T still clearly carved in medallions on the front door.[37]

How can we measure the scope and influence of Curt Teich & Co. postcards? By numbers, it's rather straightforward. When the Newberry Library, an independent research library in downtown Chicago, acquired the Curt Teich & Co. postcard collection in 2016, it assumed a catalog of 400,000 records for 15,000 unique postcards. "The core of the collection is the Records of the Curt Teich Company, which includes over 360,000 images produced by the company from 1898 and 1978, over 110,000 production files documenting the creation of the company's postcards, and additional company records," the archive's website states.[38] But that's a count of how many postcards had been saved and archived, not how many were printed over five decades of manufacture.

Records in the Curt Teich Postcard Archives indicate that a run of 6,000 was typical for a single postcard, although popular subjects and cards were often printed in runs of 12,500 or 25,000. (Some particularly popular postcards had runs of 50,000 and smaller printers presumably had smaller print runs.) "One way of reaching an estimate of at least one billion cards is to assume 100,000 individual views, each with a print run of 10,000," Meikle estimates.[39] The factory production of the postcards meant that "some one hundred thousand employees working three shifts produced millions of cards during the peak years," journalist Joni Hirsch Blackman estimates of the enterprise.[40]

What Curt Teich & Co. had done, however, was nothing short of establishing the most recognizable genre of postcard in American history, one that was imitated and copied for decades. For eighty years, Curt Teich & Co. postcards dominated Americana with their "Greetings From" script and large, blocked, bubbly letters that spelled out the names of cities in the United States. Moreover, the postcards cataloged everyday minutiae of America—hotels, schools, city buildings, and much more. Today, Curt Teich & Co. postcards circulate in a different way—through institutional archives and private collections. Contemporary online exhibitions and local histories ("Postcards Offer Colorful Look at Historical Sites," per *Argus-Leader* in Sioux Falls, South Dakota) use Curt Teich & Co. postcards as the social texts that they are.[41] The historic postcards exist as material connections to social networks of the past, building new networks of knowledge on top of their historical ones.

. . . .

"The invention of printing is the greatest event in history," Victor Hugo claimed in *The Hunchback of Notre-Dame*. "Printed thoughts are everlasting, provided with wings, intangible and indestructible."[42] Although I might be hard-pressed to consider postcards as conveying "thoughts everlasting" with the gravitas that Hugo suggests, perhaps the fact that some of the hundreds of billions of postcards that have been

U. S. Custom House, New York City.

Manhattan Bridge, New York City.

The front of the U.S. Custom House, New York City. Curt Teich & Co., issued 1913.

Manhattan Bridge, New York City. Curt Teich & Co., issued 1910.

in circulation throughout history have ended up in a family collection sitting on my desk as I type this perhaps demonstrates that print, in its many forms, does in fact endure.

Although the mass production of postcards drew—draws—on the ever-iterating interplay of paper, ink, and printing technologies, there is a unique element to postcards that sets them apart from other forms of mass printed media. Postcards depend on an individual to take them, address them, and then put them back out in the churn of ephemeral print. In order for a postcard to be, well, a postcard, it needs a person to buy it and do something with it. Postcards require participation.

The most compelling parallel to the participation that is implicit in postcards might come from completely different genres of cheap print—namely, indulgences and other printed forms that were necessary to the business of running empires. These sorts of printed media required an audience in order for the document to be actualized.

The story of Johannes Gutenberg's printing press tends to focus on his successful printing of the Bible in 1455, but in 1454 we see the earliest document printed using moveable type—a 31-line plenary indulgence, most likely printed by Gutenberg's print shop. This text is, in fact, the earliest bit of print from Gutenberg's press that has survived the ensuing centuries. Indulgences—sold by the Roman Catholic Church as a means of reducing one's stint in purgatory—became increasingly popular during the Middle Ages. In the fifteenth and sixteenth centuries, printing indulgences was so profitable that printers competed fiercely for the patents. While books were complicated to print and laborious to assemble, indulgences did not require printers to invest as much capital (time, resources, money) per item printed.

This Gutenberg-printed particular indulgence was granted by Pope Nicholas v and issued in Erfurt, Germany, on October 22, 1454. The paper has "1454" printed in Gutenberg's identifiable moveable type. But, and this is key, the indulgence has a blank space on lines 18 through 21 where the month, day, and name of the person who purchased it were to have been filled in by hand.[43] This wasn't just specific to the indulgences printed by Gutenberg. An indulgence printed on a Caxton press, for example—William Caxton introduced moveable type to England in 1476—includes the handwritten names of the recipients and the dates. "Henry Langley and his wife" and "December 13, 1476" are carefully written in by hand, thus tying people to that specific bit of print.[44] In that sense, the indulgence only became realized once the piece of printed paper was inexorably tied to its recipient. This sort of print also requires participation—it's only fully recognized when it's properly filled out.

"By providing the travelling priests with these printed forms, the promoters could dispense with the army of scribes whose wages cut into the Church's profits, and simultaneously reduce the time needed for the preparation of each Indulgence, making it possible for the priests to distribute more of them in far less time than before," historian Janet Ing Freeman explains. "Furthermore, the use of the printed forms, all closely similar in content and appearance, would ensure that each Indulgence issued would be legible and textually correct."[45] This type of item was printed on a mass scale, but it is incredibly easy to underestimate their prevalence and the scale of their network. "In 1500, the Bishop of Cefalù (in Palermo, Italy) paid for copies of more than 130,000 indulgences," historian Peter Stallybrass describes. "And the 20,000 Spanish indulgences that Jacopo Cromberger printed in 1514 and the 16,000 that he printed two years later are recorded only in notarial documents. Again, not a single copy survives."[46]

Similarly, printed forms and questionnaires quickly became a means of standardizing the flow of information during Europe's centuries of empire-building. A 1577 questionnaire was sent by King Philip of Spain to the Americas to begin to map and parse out the geography of landscapes and indigenous peoples. ("Memorandum of the things that are to be answered, and of that which shall be taken into account.") The questions were neatly printed and comprised several pages but didn't leave space for the respondent to pen in answers, although the questions on the forms clearly indicate that they were expected. ("Firstly,

Printed indulgence, Johannes Gutenberg, 1455. Height: 220 mm (8.7 in); Width: 160 mm (6.3 in). The printed indulgence—with its blank spaces—demonstrates how print requires participation.

for towns of Spaniards, state the name of the district or province in which it lies. What does this name mean in the native language, and why is it so called?" "Who was the discoverer and conqueror of this provenience? By whose order was it discovered?"[47])

Questionnaires like these were forms of claiming and mapping empires, in much the same way that pictures, portraits, and maps would be on postcards hundreds of years later. The print lay geographic claim to countries, territories, and colonies; centuries later, postcards would travel along those same lines of empire from colonies to metropoles and back again. "Ephemeral print like printed forms that were to be filled out—print that wasn't necessarily 'supposed' to be saved—can really offer insight into how empires went about their day-to-day business," explains Mitch Fraas, historian and Senior Curator of Kislak Center for Special Collections, Rare Books, and Manuscripts at the University of Pennsylvania Libraries.[48]

But this means of empire-building was possible only because of the cheap, printed forms that were readily available in Europe in the era following Gutenberg's moveable type. Very little of it has survived into the twenty-first century.

"We might begin to think that the history of printing is crucially a history of the 'blank' (that is, of printed works designed to be filled in by hand)," Peter Stallybrass suggests, a proposition which seems to suggest that the social life of print requires an active participation. Postcards, it would seem, pick up on this very specific intersection of cheap print and mass production that requires a person to act on the print. If print—especially mass-produced print—is the sum of its paper, ink, and production technologies, it is no less so the sum of its cultural contexts. Print is social and printed picture postcards were the first example of worldwide social networks.

. . . .

Back in the world of mass-produced twentieth-century postcards, I took another long look at the two Curt Teich & Co. postcards that I had found on eBay.

I was still torn about actually putting the postcards in the mail. But it didn't seem right, somehow, for those two postcards to not be in circulation, and it felt a little ridiculous to put the postcards back in their mailers and send them on to their intended recipients in envelopes. If they were truly to be postcards, I decided, I needed to fill them out. I had to laugh, imagining some future historian unearthing a 1937 postcard with a 2019 postmark and trying to figure out the sequence of events. I thought long and hard about what I would write on the back. ("Hey! This postcard was printed in 1937! Also, good luck with midterms!!!!") And then, reader, I sent the postcards.

The English Lakes.
BLEA TARN, LANGDALE.

Raphael Tuck & Sons postcard featuring "The English Lakes, Blea Tarn, Langdale." Unmailed, printed 1903–59. Raphael Tuck & Sons, Ltd. was an extremely popular London-based, early 20th-century postcard manufacturer. The company described these "oilette" postcards as "veritable miniature oil paintings."

Raphael Tuck & Sons postcard, "Kew Gardens in Summertime," printed 1903–59.

I hoped that the recipients would appreciate the gesture and the history of the artifacts. But if not, I rationalized, there are plenty more postcards where those came from.

THREE

PUBLICITY AND PROPAGANDA

....

In 1916 Yvette Borup Andrews loaded up cameras, film, paper, glass plates, and a special darkroom tent to set out as the official photographer for the American Museum of Natural History's First Asiatic Zoological Expedition.

This eighteen-month-long scientific expedition was led by Yvette's husband, Roy Chapman Andrews. (Andrews is said by some to have been the real-life inspiration for Indiana Jones.) The expedition traveled to China, Tibet, and what was then Burma, collecting zoological specimens and photographing the peoples and landscapes of Central Asia, as well as looking for fossils that could contribute to ongoing debates about hominin evolution and the origins of *Homo sapiens*. The photographs that Yvette Borup Andrews took on this expedition, as well as on the Second Asiatic Zoological Expedition in the 1920s (where scientists found dinosaur eggs at Bayanzag—the Flaming Cliffs—in Mongolia), helped create popular interest and bolster support for the American Museum of Natural History's field expeditions.

Advertisement for 3A Folding Pocket Kodak camera, 1903.

In short, photographs like hers served to create a sense of swash-buckling adventure—danger, exotic places, and travel—all in the name of science! These images offered dimensionality and authenticity to the expeditions, as well as legitimacy to the science that they were doing, in a way that a mere travelogue could not. What is significant to the story of postcards, though, are the cameras that Yvette took with her.

Specifically, she packed two Kodak 3As, a Graphic 4 × 5 tripod camera, and a more portable Graflex 4 × 5. These were standard cameras for travel, expeditions, and scientific work, and their popularity meant that the expedition would, in a pinch, most likely be able to purchase additional film or plates in other countries. "We have found after considerable field experience that the 4 × 5 is the most convenient size to handle, for the plate is large enough and can be obtained more readily than any other in different parts of the world," the Andrewses describe in their 1918 bestselling book about their travels, *Camps and Trails in China*. "The same applies to the 3A Kodak 'post-card' size film, for there are few places where foreign goods are carried that 3A films cannot be purchased."[1]

At the end of the First Asiatic Zoological Expedition, the team came home with 150 Paget color plates, 500 photographic negatives, and 10,000 feet of motion picture film, as well as over 3,000 zoological specimens for the American Museum of Natural History. Although the knowledge of which photographs from the expedition were developed onto postcards, and which of those postcards were sent to whom, has been lost to history, Yvette Borup Andrews's use of the small, portable Kodak 3A camera—where film could be loaded and unloaded in a mere matter of minutes and images developed directly onto postcard cardstock—was very much in keeping with emerging global trends in photography.

The Kodak Eastman Company was keen to put the Kodak 3A into the hands of professional and amateur photographers alike. The popularity of the camera meant that the ability to take photographs and mail them as postcards was accessible to everyone, not just professional photographers. Thus, people taking pictures—postcards, even—with their Kodak cameras managed to capture a plethora of ever-globalizing social movements, the allure of scientific expeditions, and the political throes of the first two decades of the twentieth century in a way that journalism, letters, and other written communication couldn't.

. . . .

Through her photography, Yvette Borup Andrews was helping to shape the public perception of science in early twentieth-century America, inspiring generations of scientific adventurers in the process. In effect, she created propaganda that underscored the cultural mythos of science and exploration that was influential in shaping the public perception of paleontology and natural history in the early 1900s. However, she was hardly the first photographer on a scientific expedition to do so.[2]

At its most neutral, "propaganda" simply means to "disseminate" or to "promote particular ideas," as communications scholars Garth Jowett and Victoria O'Donnell articulate in *Propaganda and Persuasion*—and people have promoted ideas and agendas for millennia. Over the last four hundred years, however, the definition of "propaganda" has become more and more pejorative—so much so that now, "to identify a message as propaganda is to suggest something negative and dishonest," Jowett and O'Donnell argue.[3]

"Propaganda may be overt or covert, black or white, truthful or mendacious, serious or humorous, rational or emotional," historian David Welch notes in the introduction to *Propaganda and Mass Persuasion: A Historical Encyclopedia, 1500 to the Present*. "Propagandists assess the context and the audience and use whatever methods and means they consider most appropriate and effective."[4] Historically, this sort of control is best done through storytelling and the crafting of narrative. And it turns out that postcards are extremely well-suited to the making and propagation of stories and narratives.

Many of the hundreds of millions of postcards commercially printed between 1900 and 1930 carried overtly political messages, whether they focused on the women's suffrage movement, armed military conflicts, nation and empire-building, or global wars. When the UK's prime minister David Lloyd George introduced the National Health Insurance Act in 1911, one of the ways that the Act was popularized was with a run of postcards, as postcards were the cheapest and most effective means of communicating with a large audience. (Historically, propaganda postcards were printed as early as the Franco-Prussian

War of 1870.) In the United States, in particular, postcards were more cost-efficient than newspapers, circulars, or any other mass-produced and mass-disseminated media.

But it's easy to lose track of individual people in the postcards of social movements and political upheavals of the early twentieth century, and the Kodak 3A camera offered people a completely different sort of propaganda. It offered a medium that they themselves could create. Everyday people could demonstrate participation in the world around them and authenticate that experience, thanks to the ability to document it and send it on in the form of a postcard. "If we can widen our terms of reference and divest propaganda of its pejorative associations, its significance as an intrinsic part of the political process in the twentieth century will be revealed," Welch offers.[5]

These postcards—"real picture" and "real photograph" postcards, as they came to be known—show that propaganda isn't always printed on a scale that is counted in the millions, but can still be pervasive enough to exist en masse. Participation in social movements and political events can be personal and, intentionally or not, creates a story, a narrative, and a mythos in the postcard that the photographer has created.

. . . .

This brings us to the technological side of real picture postcards. In order to create a real picture postcard, one needed a photographer, a camera, and specific types of paper. One also needed a darkroom or place where the photograph could be developed. But one also needed the social impetus and cachet that such a postcard medium offered, which had been established in popular culture by companies like Curt Teich & Co.

To begin with, "real picture" postcards were actual photographs. The name for this technology and postcard genre varies—sometimes called "real picture," "real photo," "real photograph," or "RPPCs"—but it was nevertheless a significant innovation in postcard history. Real postcards are made by developing a negative onto photo paper with

PREHISTORIC MAN. GOUGH'S CAVE. CHEDDAR 1376

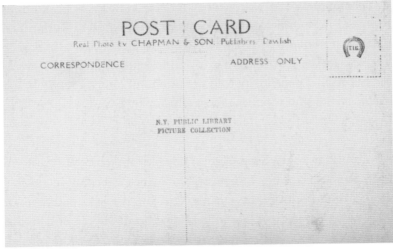

POST : CARD

Real Photo by CHAPMAN & SON. Publishers Dawlish

CORRESPONDENCE   ADDRESS ONLY

N.Y. PUBLIC LIBRARY
PICTURE COLLECTION

Real picture postcard of "prehistoric man" (9100 BP/7100 BCE) found in Gough's
Cave, Cheddar Gorge, Somerset, England. Excavated in 1903; remains currently
held at the Natural History Museum, London. Real picture postcards like this helped
spread news of scientific discoveries. Printed by Chapman & Son, Dawlish.

a pre-printed postcard backing; they were the result of chemical reactions on a light-sensitive surface or paper. The "realness" comes from putting an actual photograph on paper, rather than printing paper through inked lithographic stones, metal presses, or glass plates of printing presses.

While shooting real picture postcards might have been a more individualized way of putting a postcard into circulation, the success of the entire genre depended on the social and technological systems that supported the mass-production of cameras and film. For American real picture photographers in particular, many companies pushed the idea that—with the right camera, paper, and an "up-by-your-bootstraps" entrepreneurial gumption—it was entirely possible to make a successful business out of taking photos for and printing postcards.[6] (Turn-of-the-twentieth-century ads for Kodak played to this ethos: "Why don't you make your own postcards?" "Pick out a few of your best negatives and try a dozen postcards!"[7])

Before a photograph for a postcard could be shot and processed, photographers needed a camera that could fill the technological and social niche. And, as it turns out, there were many cameras during this time that catered to the small entrepreneur who was interested in leveraging the postcard craze into a successful extension of a photography business. ("Thanks to George Eastman, one of the authentic geniuses of the Industrial Revolution in the United States, an individual could go into the postcard business on a shoestring," historians Paul Vanderwood and Frank Samponaro suggest.[8]) Perhaps more than any other purveyor of postcard supplies at the beginning of the twentieth century, the Eastman Kodak Company "anticipated, met, and built the market for photographic postcards," historian Rosamond Vaule describes in her study of rural American real picture postcards.[9]

The Eastman Kodak Company's first foray into the personalized postcard market was in the form of the 3A Folding Pocket Kodak camera. (Other popular 3A cameras from Kodak included the folding "Brownie" camera from 1909 and the "Autographic" from 1916.) "Travel,

THE STORE OF BEACH PARK DRUG CO.   612 MIDLAND AVENUE, MIDLAND BEACH.
STATEN ISLAND, N. Y.

Postcard advertising Kodaks (and more) for sale, Staten Island, New York, c. 1910.

diplomacy, and foreign residence were subjects for the 3A camera, and Kodak's international presence facilitated the process," Vaule points out.[10] Not only was the camera ubiquitous and popular for the typical holidaygoer, it was also the go-to model for scientific expeditions of the decade, which is why it is no surprise that Yvette Borup Andrews opted to take it to Central Asia. Other real picture postcard photographers used the camera extensively.

The Eastman camera had a fixed-focus lens of 57 millimeters focal length and an aperture stop of f/9. The original box camera Kodak produced measured 3.5 × 3.75 × 6.5 inches—it was of a size that could slip into a pocket or a camera bag. The entire apparatus cost $25 (roughly $735 in 2020), and the purchase included enough film and processing time to produce a hundred images. The idea was that an amateur photographer would shoot a roll of film and send the camera back to Rochester, New York, where the film would be removed, and the images processed onto paper to produce photographic prints. The camera was then sent back to its owner and the process would begin again.

By 1902, however, George Eastman had narrowed the focus of the Kodak personal cameras and was able to streamline the process of developing photographs so that customers didn't have to send in their cameras. Instead the Eastman Kodak Company issued postcard-size photographic paper that meant images could be developed straight onto postcards. And by 1903 a newer and cheaper 3A model had entered the market—a "bellows" camera that cost $2 (close to $60 today). The film negatives for the 3A were the perfect dimensions to make postcard-size prints. A 1911 advertisement for the camera praised "its applicability to post-card photography, but also for the unusually effective landscape views that it yields horizontally and the beautifully proportioned full length portraits, vertically."[11]

Camera thus in hand, the next step in the real picture postcard process would be to develop the image onto a physical card. Kodak offered photographers several options. Photographers could, of course, send in the film and Kodak would take care of the process. Between 1906 and 1910, Kodak offered factory processing and printing for 10 cents (or $2.93 today) per negative and local camera shops across the United States were quick to advertise that they could and would develop postcards taken with Eastman Kodaks.[12] Or, following in the trend set by the personal cameras, photographers could handle the process themselves—and the new paper and techniques for developing real picture postcards meant that it was more than feasible to undertake this as an amateur. Not only was it possible, but Kodak encouraged it.

One of the significant technological developments for putting these small-scale personalized postcards into the mail centered around the new Velox postcard paper stock that the Eastman Kodak Company produced. Most cardstock papers were chemically treated with gelatin silver to receive the film image. The other side of the paper was printed with the traditional postcard format: heading, stamp box, and divided back. According to a 1903 catalog of Kodak supplies, "Velox postal cards [meaning postcards printed on Velox paper] may be sent through the mail by affixing a stamp on the address side. Sensitized on the back and have a surface suitable for writing upon. They make delightful souvenirs for travelers to send to their friends." The advertisement continues to tout how easy it was to simply pop a picture postcard in the post. One could readily print on Velox postcards in the evening at one's hotel, and the following morning they could be written upon and mailed. In this respect they were especially advantageous to the touring amateur who had taken along her Kodak camera and developing machine.[13]

Although Velox and Azo were Kodak's most popular papers, Kodak also produced blueprint, sepia, and cyanotype paper stock that, in the twenty-first century, looks to be the iconic embodiment of "old-timey" looking images. Other papers produced by non-Kodak companies offered different finishes—glossy, semi-matte, and studio (a velvet surface). Advertisements for printing various real picture postcards were featured in local papers across the United States. In August 1907, for example, *The Post-Star* of Glens Falls, New York, ran an ad that priced "blue print" postcards at 15 cents a dozen. Velox and Ayo postcards were priced at two dozen for 25 cents.[14] As fast as photographers bought cameras and printed postcards, new type of paper, film, or techniques were introduced for them to try.

But making real picture postcards required developing pictures as well as a camera, film, and paper. On the First Asiatic Expedition, Yvette Borup Andrews carried a collapsible rubber darkroom made by the Abercrombie & Fitch Co., about 7 feet high and 4 feet in diameter (215 × 120 cm), in which to develop her photographs. (In the early twentieth century the company was a serious outfitter for expeditions. Abercrombie & Fitch equipped the American president Theodore Roosevelt's 1909 African safari as well as Admiral Richard Byrd's 1928 expedition to Antarctica.) Yvette's darkroom was incredibly versatile and was built to deal with tough field conditions as it "could be hung from the limb of a tree or the rafters of a building and be ready for use in five minutes."[15] She set up her "little rubber darkroom", as the press called it, "in any convenient tree branch, wherever she pleased, and developed

Kodak as you go.

Eastman Kodak Co., Rochester, N. Y., *The Kodak City*

Kodak's early 20th-century advertising focused on the
portability of their cameras. This ad from *Photoplay* (January 1921),
shows a skiing couple with a Kodak folding camera.

[the expedition's] pictures in temperatures of 105 in the shade, with a
humidity of 150."[16]

Not everyone who developed postcards, however, needed something
as robust and rugged as that. Although Kodak offered a developing
machine to its customers as early as 1903, that system required postcards to be developed in "the old way, in the dark-room."[17] The ROC
(Rochester Optical Company) Post Card Printer was targeted toward
the small-time photographer either printing postcards for personal use
(making postcards from their own touristy travel) or making small-run

batches of individualized postcards (a family portrait, a commemorative photograph: something personal and not available on a commercially large scale.) Photographers would drop the card into place in the printer box—against the negative—and pull a lever. This would expose the negative, transfer the image to the postcard cardstock, and not require the messiness of a darkroom or laboratory.

"The ROC Post Card Printer is made for the man who desires an inexpensive, yet rapid and trustworthy machine for printing developing out post cards," ran an ad by the Rochester Optical Company in the May 1910 issue of *Kodak Trade Journal*, apparently overlooking the possibility that women were also making real picture postcards and had been for years.[18] The ROC printer could develop postcard photographs with either natural or artificial light. Other machines quickly came on the market that allowed developers to add type-print to cards (for example, a date and a location) as well as to "double print" postcards to achieve an oval frame or vignette style. A non-Kodak printing product from Britain—called the Graber—was advertised as a "well-established and famous post card machine . . . in use in all parts of the world, giving entire satisfaction." The Graber printed text as well as photographs onto rolls of postcard paper and then snipped the scrolls into individual postcards. Potential customers were reminded that it could "be worked either by hand or by motor."[19]

Kodak even commissioned sets of real picture postcards to hype real picture postcards; these cards, popular between 1908 and 1916, featured the "Kodak Girls," who posed with Kodak cameras in their Edwardian-era garb. Unsurprisingly, George Eastman—and the Kodak company—moved to aggressively patent anything and everything associated with their cameras, photographs, and postcards. (The back of Kodak's real picture postcards were Kodak postcard paper stock stamped with the company's name.) Eastman referred to the non-professional photographer and postcard maker as a "Kodaker."[20]

Kodak wasn't the only company to jump on marketing this activity as a career for entrepreneurs. An advertisement for the Chicago-based

International Metal & Ferrotype Co. in *The Masses* in July 1914 talked up the self-empowerment of becoming an independent postcard photographer as it publicized their camera and printing setup, the Diamond Post Card Gun. It had a cannon-shaped body made of nickel and a velvet "dark cloth" for the photographer to step under; the entire thing was mounted on a wooden tripod. "Follow the creed of your calling, join the ranks of big money makers. Be independent. Get out of the salary rut, piling up money for the capitalists," the advertisement encouraged. "Get into a business of your own where you can easily make $25.00 a day and up."[21] The International Metal & Ferrotype Co. promised aspiring entrepreneurs that "no experience was needed" to operate the Post Card Gun—just a willingness, one presumes, to shoot photographs.

. . . .

All of this begs the question: Given the technology and social opportunity to create their own propaganda, what did people take pictures of? In short, anything and everything.

If Instagram is our twenty-first-century parallel to the world of postcards—real picture postcards, in particular—then we would expect to see twentieth-century postcards of food, pets, slogans or quotes, friends, and of course, selfies. And by and large, this is what we see in real picture postcards taken to send to friends and family: A glamorous vacation. A Votes for Women banner hung in a town's Main Street. Family portraits, both formal and candid. Pretty much anything and everything that has been stuffed into an Instagram feed was photographed, printed, and mailed as a postcard more than a century earlier.

In 2016 communications scholars Pavica Sheldon and Katherine Bryant argued that Instagram was the fastest-growing social network site globally. When they surveyed college students about why and how the students used Instagram, they found that some who were very socially active—students who traveled, went to sporting events, visited with friends, and so on—were much more likely to post photographs and stories to Instagram to document what they were doing. When Sheldon

ADMIRAL JELLICOE LANDING AT SUVA, FIJI.   HARRY GARDINER

Lami River, near Suva,, Fiji.   26.

Admiral Jellicoe landing at Suva, Fiji. Photograph by Harry Gardiner, published by "The Rose Stereographs," Armadale, Victoria. 1919. Labelled "Real Photo" on verso.

Lami River, near Suva, in Fiji. Printed on verso: "Real photo postcard, British made. Caine series, Suva, Fiji. Copyright."

Real picture postcard from Camp Fremont, California; author's great-grandfather
George Sandberg, third from right, and army unit, 1918. The postcard was
trimmed down from its original postcard-printed size to fit in a picture frame,
rather than serve as a piece of mailed correspondence.

and Bryant probed students on the question of whether Instagram
contributed to overall narcissism, they found that students generally
used Instagram to "look cool" or, as the researchers put it, to "surveille"
their peers. A 2020 estimate suggests that over 100 million pictures and
videos are posted to Instagram every day, all to be shared, liked, and
acknowledged by its 500 million-plus active daily users. This social
performance trades on the same cachet of social networking of earlier
mass mediums—and we've simply exchanged postcards for pixels.[22]

Perhaps, though, the most interesting part of the overlap between
the two social networks is what they share in the world of publicity and
propaganda and the means by which they circulate it. It's not hard to
think of postcards as propaganda when they're printed on a massive scale
and carry overt messages—that the sender is either for or against some

nationalist, feminist, or patriotic movement and wants to convey that sentiment to the receiver. And certainly collectors' or archival catalogs of postcards show that such sponsored messages were devised, printed, and mailed by the hundreds of thousands. The social and technological machinery built up to produce postcards on a large scale at the turn of the twentieth century had any number of themes, motifs, and images that businesses paid postcard manufacturers to print, and this top-down model meant that postcard motifs were set by people other than those who were buying the postcards.

There might be an argument that "the market"—such as it is—determined the range of postcards for sale during this era. But unless people controlled their own means of production, it was difficult for consumers to send any sort of postcard other than what postcard companies thought they ought to buy, collect, or put in the mail.

And this is where real photograph postcards became particularly powerful propaganda in the early twentieth century—in the decades of massive global events like the women's suffrage movements, wars, and international conflicts. Real picture postcards were a means of creating, curating, and circulating an individual's experience and point of view.

. . . .

When the Mexican Revolution broke out in 1910, it was the beginning of a long and brutal conflict. It stemmed from issues of presidential succession of President Porfirio Díaz following a contested vote in 1910, although there had been smoldering labor disputes and strikes for years prior. In June 1906, for example, there was a violent labor strike at the Consolidated Copper Mining Company in Cananea, Sonora, where 23 Mexicans and Americans died. The strike was captured by a postcard photographer who created a series of twenty undivided-back postcards that offer a window into the pre-Revolution labor tensions in Mexico. The photographer (whose name is lost to history) managed to capture a shot of Colonel W. C. Greene—the American mine manager—addressing a restless crowd of Mexican workers. Disputes like this—as well as the 1910 Mexican presidential election—quickly became the catalyst for political revolution.

In a twist of irony, however, this was good news for American postcard manufacturers. American photographers who attached themselves and their portable postcard-printing cameras to the conflict offered a perspective and lens to document the decade between 1910 and 1920. These postcard images were often spontaneous, unstaged photographs that, in no small way, depended upon a photographer's luck in snapping a candid shot. The idea that amateurs could successfully step into the business of taking and making postcards was directly promoted by camera companies themselves.[23]

Postcard images kept pace with Mexico's civil war and the involvement of the United States. As American troops mobilized along the border—part of what American history would call the "Border War" or "Border Campaign," nominally to protect American citizens and economic interests along the border—Americans' appetite for postcards of the conflict proved to be insatiable. In fact, over one hundred firms and individuals would seize the opportunity to capitalize on the craze, producing tens of thousands of postcards over the next six years, with sales peaking in 1916.

In that year, the same year in which Yvette Borup Andrews took her cameras and went to Central Asia, an American photographer in El Paso, Walter H. Horne, leveraged his proximity to the United States' border with Mexico to build up a lucrative postcard business. His niche? Catering to American soldiers and tourists eager to send postcards "back home" that featured pictures of the Mexican Revolution. Horne's postcards—his real picture postcards, that is—served to codify how many Americans came to think of the Mexican Revolution. His postcard images were more widely circulated than anything printed in a newspaper of the time and shaped how many Americans envisioned the conflict.

By all accounts, when Horne moved to El Paso to treat his tuberculosis in 1910, he had little interest and no experience in photography before setting up a studio in town. However, when he joined his fellow El Pasoans in "attending" border skirmishes, Horne began to consider the unique picture postcard market that El Paso offered: The town was so close to the border that its residents could see combat in Ciudad Juárez, Chihuahua.

It took almost two and a half years for Horne's picture postcard business to become profitable and it wasn't until the second battle of Ciudad Juárez in mid-November 1913 that Horne started selling postcards by the tens of thousands. By April 1914 business was good enough that Horne spent $135 (approximately $3,500 today) on a new Eastman Kodak Graflex camera to supplement his (presumed) Kodak 3A. One technological advantage that the Graflex had over the 3A was that it could use cut film for negatives that could be exposed in single frames and processed onto postcards immediately; the rolled film of a 3A camera had to be cut before it was processed. Many real picture postcards were

Tourist postcard from Ciudad Juárez, printed contemporaneously with the real picture postcards of the Mexican Revolution.

printed as individual mementos, but some photographers, like Horne, were able to leverage their images into picture postcards. Although Horne's postcards were printed in the thousands, they weren't printed on the industrial scale of Curt Teich & Co.—however, Horne's post-cards were definitely circulated.

By May of 1914 Horne had shipped 7,800 postcards to New York City and had standing orders for 16,000 more. In December 1915 Horne invested the postcard profits in a photography studio business and part-nership with Henry E. Cottman. The postcard side of the business was called the "Mexican War Photo Postcard Company" and had its own letterhead and stationery; the business lasted until Horne's death in 1921. By just about every metric imaginable, Horne was the most financially successful photographer of the Mexican Revolution and the associated American military activity along the international border.

On March 21, 1916, Horne wrote a letter back home informing his family that he had produced an astounding 2,700 postcards that day; by early August of 1916, he could boast a daily production of 5,000 cards. The most popular postcards were generally battle scenes, of course, but his images of executions and jingoistic stereotypes of Mexicans also proved to be bestsellers. (Other popular photographic postcards by other printers featured portraits of Mexico's leaders, American troops, or refugees.) Postcards like these would seem to offer a glimpse into world events that would have felt very removed from everyday life that wasn't on the border.

Images on Horne's real picture postcards alternate between the surreal, the banal, and the horrifying. For some Americans, the conflict was a spectacle, and Horne's postcards from El Paso show Americans perched on rooftops of buildings such as hotels—many women sporting parasols—to watch the armed skirmishes. One postcard from May 1911 shows groups of Americans, bedecked out in their full finery, picnicking by the Rio Grande while watching the conflict play out in front of them. They had arrived en masse via the city's streetcars, which had been rerouted to deliver them to the area. (The mayor of El Paso, Charles E.

Kelly, issued a warning that Mauser bullets would "rain on the banks of the Rio Grande." Despite Kelly's warnings, El Paso's streetcars had to be roped off in order to limit the number of people they could bring to the waterfront.) These postcards—which show how Americans watched the Mexican Revolution as spectators—offer a unique glimpse at the history of how people see conflict. And, since these images were printed on postcards, the seller was offering that perspective back to the buyer.

The postcards were unendingly popular with American troops, which brings us to Horne's carefully curated and perpetuated postcard propaganda. Horne (and other postcard printers) focused on posed action shots and staged images of "exotic" animals such as rattlesnakes. They also showed burned and charred bodies. Executions. Graves. Violence and racial stereotypes. Bodies—Mexican bodies—left in the desert. Postcards of the Texas Rangers were posed to create a portrait of law and order along the border between the United States and Mexico. Postcard photographs show that funerals of American soldiers were stately, solemn processions where caskets were draped with American flags. The picture postcards showed refugees from the conflict—some American, most Mexican. Postcards that featured multiple pictures of Pancho Villa's corpse proved to be very popular. There were jocular attempts at levity that fall particularly flat when looking at the postcards over a hundred years later.

Photographs—particularly those printed on postcards—offer an implied authenticity and this feeling is certainly what photographers like Horne counted on to generate interest in their postcards. What you're seeing on a postcard is "real," the logic implies, because a photograph isn't something that's open to artistic interpretation. According to this logic, the photograph documents, the viewer interprets. Following this reasoning, photographic postcards of the Mexican Revolution could be internalized simply as journalism—a photographer documenting what he (invariably a he, as far as the images on border postcards can be traced to a specific photographer) saw along the border and how the Mexican Revolution looked to an American there to make money from selling his photo postcards. The real picture was, well, what recipients thought was "real"—and also what they considered to be authentic.

But postcard photographs can be untrue, unreal, and misleading on many levels—especially when an image is pirated and reprinted. One of Horne's more macabre postcard scenes was of a hanging in Mexico. In the picture, two Mexican men are shown being hanged from a tree as a bandolier-sporting, sombrero-wearing, rifle-carrying Mexican soldier looks on, with three white Americans in the background. The postcard is titled "Execution in Mexico." Horne's original postcard image, however, was pirated by H. H. Stratton, who bought a Horne original copy of the "Execution" for a couple of cents and then made a copy negative of the card and changed the scene. (Stratton was "one of the more notorious pirates of the period," historians Vanderwood

"Villa's Camp Near Juarez." Real picture collage of scenes from the Mexican Revolution, 1914. Postcards like this functioned like contemporary photojournalism, curating "authentic" and carefully constructed images to be sent around the world. Names of individuals unknown. Unknown postcard printer, contemporary of Walter Horne.

"Refugees at the border—awaiting admission to the U.S." Postcard collage of scenes
from the Mexican Revolution, 1914. Names of individuals unknown.
Unknown postcard printer, contemporary of Walter Horne.

"Zapata's Rebels destroying R.R. bridge." Postcard collage of scenes from Mexican Revolution,
1914. Names of individuals unknown. Unknown postcard printer, contemporary of Walter Horne.

and Samponaro note.[24]) Stratton removed the three Americans from the card as well as the left hand of one of the victims. The card is darker (both in racist stereotype as well as literal hue) and Stratton retitled the card as "Familiar Scene in Mexico during the Revolution of the Past Three Years."

The camera lens isn't neutral. American-produced images of the conflict ranged from documenting the everyday mundane details of village life (on both sides of the border) to outright racism, stoking American fears of immigrants and pandering to stereotypes of Mexico. On one hand it would appear that Horne's photographs offered early photojournalism coverage of the war—photographs taken on the scene were seemingly empirically valid—but this argument is easily countered by remembering that he was running a money-making enterprise. He wasn't there to document the conflict and its social ramifications. He was there to sell postcards. And, more specifically, to sell postcards to Americans who were going to send them around the United States.

. . . .

Walter Horne wasn't alone in his realization that "real picture" or "real photo" postcards were able to connect postcards with current events. Before bumper stickers, the "like" button, and viral hashtags, postcards were the most ubiquitous means of creating awareness about a social movement. And few social movements did this with more political savvy and ferocity than the early twentieth-century suffrage campaigns in the United States and the United Kingdom.

Between 1908 and 1920 there were over 1,000 unique suffrage-themed postcards—both pro- and anti-movement—issued in America. (These include real picture postcards as well as many printed on lithographic presses.) British activists produced at least double that number, thanks in no small part to presses specifically dedicated to producing such cards. Both countries' suffragists drew heavily on imagery that shocked audiences (such as cartoon depictions of suffragists' torture by police); photographs of rallies, demonstrations, and leaders; and allegorical art.

From the mid-1800s early suffrage movements to the adopting of the Nineteenth Amendment in the United States in 1920, which prohibited states and the federal government from denying someone the right to vote based on sex, postcards were conveniently sold everywhere from stationery and drug stores to newsstands and souvenir boutiques.[25]

Suffrage at this time wasn't so much a single movement as a collection of different trends. While the main goal of nineteenth- and early twentieth-century suffragists in the U.S. and UK was to advocate for women's right to vote, there was a plethora of different axes along which different groups aligned themselves. In the American suffrage movement, for example, there were differences between regional and national chapters of the suffrage movement, how class featured in socioeconomic lines, and issues of race. Most prominent advocating came from white women, often at the expense of Black women.

Although the question of universal suffrage has been taken up many times over the past several centuries, it was particularly politically urgent in the decades leading up to the First World War. In the United States, women's suffrage was recognized with the Nineteenth Amendment to the Constitution, which guaranteed women the right to vote and was formally ratified on August 18, 1920. In the United Kingdom, women's right to vote was guaranteed through two different acts of Parliament in 1918 and 1928. (The question of women's suffrage is still far from globally settled. Kuwait, for example, first allowed women to vote in 1999; this right was revoked before being reinstated in 2005. And as recently as 2015, Saudi Arabia allowed women to vote for the first time in the kingdom's modern history.)

The suffrage movements understood the value of postcards. As early as the 1860s, suffragist organizers were making and sending an awful lot of postcards. (These were all privately printed, rather than being printed by the United States government.) One of the earliest suffrage postcards ("pioneer cards" in collectors' parlance) announced a meeting on Thursday, December 16, 1886, in celebration of Mrs. Lucy C. Barber's casting an illegal vote in her hometown of Alfred Centre, New York.

(She was arrested. The abolitionist and writer Harriet Beecher Stowe's sister, Isabella Beecher Hooker, attended the celebration and promptly founded the Connecticut Woman Suffrage Association.) The last line on the card—"Admit Bearer and Friends"—illustrates that the card wasn't just to inform recipients about the meeting, but would serve as a ticket for entry.

But pioneer cards proved difficult for the suffrage movements, as they weren't very versatile, and the U.S. government had issued prohibitions against writing anything other than addresses on the backs of early postcards. When government regulations eased a bit in 1898 and "Private Mailing Cards" were introduced to the Americans—as well as the Rural Free Delivery system—postcards, especially real picture postcards, became an integral part of the suffrage movements.

Across the globe, suffrage movements spent decades systematically commissioning, designing, printing, mailing, and collecting postcards as a particularly powerful part of various suffrage movements. Suffragist propaganda was well-honed, well-placed, and well-timed. Various chapters and organizations, both in America and the UK, used local printers for postcards to create personal mementos for women participating in local suffrage events. Images of national events, portraits of the movement's leaders, and propaganda were produced on a much larger scale than one photographer with a camera could possibly achieve.

"Since the local newspaper did not print pictures and the larger postcard manufacturers scorned views of purely local interest and limited sales potential, small postcard producers played an important role in capturing America on film during the first and second decades of the twentieth century," historians Vanderwood and Samponaro point out, describing the function of these real photo postcards regardless of whether they contained pictures of the Mexican Revolution or women's suffrage movements. The social niche was the same.[26]

Because postcards are, by nature, so ephemeral, it is impossible to estimate how many non-mass-produced suffrage postcards were made, delivered, and collected. For individuals using local photography studios and the first personal, hand-held cameras, printing photographs of themselves participating in the social movement was very much akin to the selfies of the twenty-first century, affirming a personal connection to a particular time and place. But official postcards were also produced to bring attention to the question of voting rights for American women. In her report about the memorabilia and merchandizing of the suffrage movement at the National American Woman Suffrage Association's meeting in 1916, Esther G. Ogden clearly stated, "We exist for two purposes—to serve the suffrage cause throughout the country and to prove that we can serve that cause and also develop a successful business."[27]

For over a decade, new suffrage postcards were advertised in the *Women's Journal*, with many special-issue postcards serving as fundraisers. In 1913 prominent American suffragette Lydia Gray advertised in the *Women's Journal* that she would take any suffrage quotation sent to her and turn it into a postcard; she produced five such cards, printed on bark-looking cardstock, with quotes from Julia Ward Howe and Susan B. Anthony. Supporters could buy two of the cards for a nickel. The suffrage movement also packaged together postcards and postcard collections that could be purchased cheaply, with the purchaser able to contribute to the cause with even a penny postcard.[28]

Iconic suffragist moments in the United States and the UK were particularly suitable for picture postcards. In 1913 the Long Island socialite Rosalie Jones ("General" Rosalie Jones, per the press at the time) had led a march for women's suffrage—a pilgrimage, really—of 295 miles from New York to Washington, DC, just prior to Woodrow Wilson's inauguration as president of the United States. The idea was that the sixteen-day march would end just after the inauguration, and the suffrage marchers would request an audience with Wilson, with the idea of urging him to support a federal amendment specifically authorizing women's suffrage. (Such an amendment wouldn't happen for another six years.) The march was highly publicized and many of the hikers financed their way from New York to Washington by selling memorabilia and souvenirs along the way.

VOTES FOR WOMEN

First prize in Vineland parade.

The Procession Passing Stand of N. A. W. S. A.

Postcard image of women and girls riding a "Votes for Women" float in Vineland, New Jersey, 1914. Real picture postcards created a connection between an event and the person buying or sending the postcard. Names of individuals unknown.

Women's suffrage procession in Washington, DC, printed 1913. Names of individuals unknown.

They also had their pictures taken, and these pictures were rapidly turned into real picture postcards. "One advantage to the Real Photo card is that it was virtually immediate," historian Kenneth Florey explains. "People attending an event . . . could buy a postcard picturing it and send it to friends even before they left town to come home."[29] One such "real photo" postcard—dated February 28, 1913—shows women finishing the march, holding American flags in coats, hats, and cloaks to ward off the chill of the winter day. Rosalie Jones is front and center. The caption of the postcard, printed in white across the bottom of the image, reads "Pilgrims Entering Washington, D.C." in shaky handwriting. The real photo postcard offers a "realness" to the historical moment that a postcard with a cartoon or a sketch simply couldn't. When the Nineteenth Amendment was finally passed in 1919, a plethora of postcards commemorated Alice Paul's "Silent Sentinels," who had paraded outside the White House gates from January 1917 to June 1919.

Across the Atlantic, real picture postcards offered similar captured moments of marches, protests, parades, pageantry, and the like. Photographers—suffragist and non-suffragist alike—captured images from pilgrimages and bazaars; others documented the release of suffrage prisoners and any local event across the nation that could hold some sort of political or social purchase. (It goes without saying, of course, that all of the local and national chapters of various suffrage organizations in the UK also relied on postcards with art, quotes, cartoons, and images that would drum up support for the cause.) Photographers also documented the more militant history of the women's suffrage movement across the UK. One postcard depicts a still-smoldering fire—started by suffragists—at the prime minister's house in April 1913. Ten uniformed officers stand outside the residence, manning a fire hose that is turned on the house, with its broken windows and scorched exterior.

"What appeared to fascinate many English were the scenes of suffrage destruction," Florey argues in *Women's Suffrage Memorabilia*, "such as the burning of Roughwood House, the fire at Hurst Park . . . the attack on the Nevill Cricket Ground . . . the conflagration at the prime minister's house at Levitleigh, St. Leonards, and the destruction of several churches . . . Anti-suffragists took revenge, and their actions can be seen on several cards depicting the wreckage of the suffrage headquarters in Bristol."[30] Again, postcards—physical items that could be bought, sent, and collected as single messages or amassed as part of a collection dedicated to a cause—were not insignificant.

From the more militant side of the suffragette movement in the UK, the post—in addition to images on postcards themselves—became part of the Votes for Women movement. "In the archive, we have the story of Miss Soloman and Miss McLellan, who posted themselves to the Prime Minister Herbert Asquith on the 23rd of February 1909," the Postal Museum in London explains. "At the time the Post Office allowed individuals to be posted by express messenger. They were however not allowed admittance to No. 10 Downing Street and instead the poor telegraph messenger boy A. S. Palmer was in trouble for not acquiring a signature for delivery."[31]

Women's suffrage movements were not the only organizations to mobilize postcards to their advantage. The anti-suffrage movement was more than capable of producing every imaginable meme and misogynistic message on postcards to be printed and mailed. Various anti-suffrage movements did not take suffrage propaganda lying down and, in the decades leading up to various governments formalizing voting rights, the anti-suffragists created their own raft of cards that furthered their own narrative and agenda.

On a global scale, anti-suffrage propaganda sought to feed on several fears. Communications scholar and postcard historian Catherine Palczewski suggests that first and foremost was the fear that men would be "feminized" as a result of women being allowed to vote. Other popular anti-suffrage motifs traded on unflattering stereotypes of harpy-like suffragettes and "naïve but attractive ingénues" who were simply in over their heads with all of the muss and fuss of figuring out how to vote. The suffrage movement, these groups argued through their blunt propaganda, were out to sacrifice hearth and home for the right to vote.

Postcard of Emmeline Pethick Lawrence with her signature, c. 1907.

The images on anti-suffrage postcards played on these social fears in vivid detail. In both American and British examples, common themes emerged: "comic" violence against activists; the haplessness of women in politics; the suffering of children, neglected by women who no longer cared for them; and, last but certainly not least, the emasculation of men who were already able to vote and closely guarded that as their patriarchal right.

MRS. PANKHURST.
(Founder of the Women's Social and Political Union.)

Real picture postcard of Emmeline Pankhurst, c. 1907.

In the world of suffrage postcards, real picture cards offered a way for suffragists and anti-suffragists alike to shape, create, and frame narratives that were far more personal than any printed out in a factory by the tens of thousands. "Postcards were ubiquitous, cheap, easily accessible, and clearly participated in the suffrage controversy in a way that developed and extended the argument beyond what can be found in the verbal argument contained in broadsides and print media," Palczewski offers.[32]

The personalization of propaganda tied people to a social movement in ways that hadn't happened in the decades of postcard history that preceded it.

. . . .

In an era where photojournalism was nascent at best, real picture postcards and "printed photo postcards" (postcards printed at a slightly larger scale) seemed to offer an authenticity that their contemporary cartoon-laden propaganda postcards did not. "While they were commercial products, they were also individual, eloquent works that reflected American life and values," Rosamond Vaule points out.[33] And this was true around the world. What the receiver of the card saw was real, the logic went, because the camera was an objective tool to document events. Many of these real picture postcards were propaganda—powerful propaganda at that.

Postcard propaganda reflected local expressions of global phenomena by personalizing and catering to expectations. But the introduction of personal printing offered the possibility for individual people to capture personal narratives and stories that were part of larger social movements or global conflicts. For photographers like Yvette Borup Andrews, Walter Horne, and a plethora of unrecorded photographers of various social movements, this was a question of technology and society co-existing and co-evolving.

While the history of postcards is certainly a history of mass production, cameras such as the Kodak 3A and the larger Graflex reframed (as it were) the question of who could make a postcard and put that specific card into circulation together with the billions of others that were mailed around the world. But even on an individual level, the technology of putting real scenes on actual postcards reinforced social and political narratives; the camera was only as objective as the photographer taking the picture.

FOUR

HAVING A WONDERFUL TIME, WISH YOU WERE HERE

....

In 1990 the Klein Postcard Service of Boston launched a postcard series to let the city's tourists know that lobster was definitely a thing in Boston. In a push to show visitors that Boston was home to some seriously fine seafood and not just all those "boring history" factoids that had graced Klein's Boston postcards for decades, the company opted for an unconventional, humorous campaign that used a series of cards to impress upon visitors the serious responsibility of purchasing and consuming crustaceans while visiting the city. With a picture of a hapless lobster on the front of the card, the back read:

> Lobster is big in Boston: by city ordinance visitors to Boston
> must not only order a lobster dinner, but they must write home
> about it. A post card picturing a lobster may be substituted
> for a letter, but phone calls for this purpose do not satisfy the
> law. Although opposed by post card sellers, legislation to allow
> faxing lobster photos to fulfill this requirement is pending.[1]

The quirky lobster card highlights the proscriptive role that post-cards play in any tourist experience and have done over the last century and a half. If you are going to go through all of the trouble of actually

(No. 26)   The great wall (Peiping).   城 長 里 萬

Postcard mailed from China to Robert Boles, 1936.
The postcard illustration of the Great Wall shows an iconic bit of history and
architecture that a tourist might be expected to want to send back home.

going to a place, the logic went, why not show your friends and family
that you were there? And what could be more natural than the place
you're visiting telling you what you ought to do and see? It was the, "If
a person went on vacation, but never proved to their social circle that
they were there—did they really go?" of tourism performance.

For the last century and a half, postcards have been a way to validate
travel and to connect sender and recipient, and to connect both to a
specific geographic place. For Western tourists, they have also been a way
of commodifying particular places and making them into "recognizable"
tourist attractions. Postcards showed off international places the sender
had visited, and were also how urban citizens around the world were
drawn to off-the-beaten-path rural destinations in the early twentieth
century. Many of these rural destinations offered real picture postcards

of their main streets, town squares, local businesses, and even land-scapes. In the United States, these rural postcards—real picture as well as small-run commercially printed postcards—revitalized the United States Post Office by increasing the amount of stamped mail sent through rural postal routes. For popular tourist destinations, commercially printed postcards were made by the hundreds of millions and offered a carefully curated image of a place.

More important than the specific type of postcards that were sent, however, were the social ramifications of sending a postcard. Postcards have been part of the social life of tourism for the last hundred or so years. They have played an important role in how one "ought" to be a tourist, whether traveling domestically or internationally. Not only should tourists send postcards back home, but they can collect postcards to keep from their travels as souvenirs.

For many early twentieth-century tourists, postcards were an im-portant part of the experience. Guidebooks like the famous Baedeker series explained to Western tourists how they ought to visit Europe and what they should see. Sending postcards back home proved that they had participated in that bit of travel performance. Sets of postcards from abroad were also the stuff of collectors' albums, and could serve as personal mementos of a trip. (Mark Twain, for example, kept a set of postcards from his trip to Warwick Castle in England after the Baedeker guide recommended that he see it.) With the rise of middle-class tourism in the twentieth century on both sides of the Atlantic, postcards became a ubiquitous bit of material culture associated with travel.[2]

What's especially striking about the Boston lobster postcards of the 1990s is how they cast Boston in a completely different tourist light than postcards from a mere fifteen years earlier. Picture postcards from Boston show that in 1977, Boston was depicted as "a center of heritage and science and technology."[3] By 1990 more postcards featured sightseeing and emphasized shopping and academia. How a city is por-trayed—and the messages that a postcard buyer, sender, and recipient take from the image that's on the postcard—are a means of curating a city's reputation. And, over time, how a place is imagined, remembered, photographed, and commodified changes.

"By connecting the place a postcard is sent from and the place it is sent to, the postal journey made by a postcard is its most obvious spatial feature," historians Jean-Christophe Foltête and Jean-Baptiste Litot describe. "A postcard displayed on a rack is associated with a first geographical location, which is the site featured in the photograph. It is also associated with a second location, which is the tourist site at which it is on sale."[4]

Postcards, more than any other sort of souvenir, have served as tourism's main material currency since the nineteenth century.

. . . .

For thousands of years, humans have been visiting places that they do not call home. In ancient Mesopotamia, for example, around 3000 BCE, rulers and nobles enacted laws that specifically protected roads for travelers and for building waystations to facilitate travel within their realms. And while Babylonian and Assyrian cuneiform tablets captured some of the excitement as well as the headache of travel, they tended to focus on the issues of coordinating transit and merchandise. It's hard, to say the least, to imagine that the trials and travails of these travels were acts of pure leisure.

> Tell Amur-ilī: Addu sends the following message:
> From here I will go to the town of Burušhattum, together with the assistants of Ah-šalim, according to your instruction . . .
> Ennānum has not yet arrived here; he is staying in the town of Tikurna.
> Do not be angry with me for my delaying. Send me a donkey-load of tin and have it transported (into the town Burušhattum) by the man Urā. Make up your mind, there, about your *sallam* donkey's meeting with me in Burušattum so your decision (in the matter) can reach me (in time).

Please, dear brother, do not make me act on my own responsibility. The police stations are very strict (at the moment).

I plan to depart within five days.

Here death has proven to be a downright inconvenience for Usûpišqum, who has been tasked with locating some errant silver:

A message from Usûpišqum: Tell Āmur-ilī and Puzur-Ištar:

I keep hearing reports that you have sent merchandise to Ina-Sin and to Inarawe. Both these men are dead! Although I searched for evidence for the arrival of any silver, there isn't any. One of you should come here from where you are, or else the silver belonging to your father will be lost.[5]

Tourism implies travel, but travel does not necessarily imply tourism. Travel is often considered a necessity; tourism is a luxury. Tourism implies a separation of business from leisure activities. (Traveling for enjoyment can be traced historically to ancient Egypt around 1500 BCE; some historians credit this to the ubiquity of chariots that made it easier to cover large distances.[6]) The Middle Ages saw a rise in pilgrimages as devout worshipers traveled to different shrines that had overt religious significance. And much of modern tourism can be traced to the Eurocentric idea of a Grand Tour across Europe, an idea that began in the mid-1600s and continued in popularity over the next two centuries.

With the advent of a European transcontinental railroad, the Grand Tour became less of a demonstration of wealth and privilege. Tourism caught on among more of the emerging Western middle class, from the United States and the United Kingdom to northern Europe and South America. Different routes became more formalized, the stops along the way were predictable, and the journey became more and more accessible. By the 1900s a lot of the social performance of tourism had become a rote

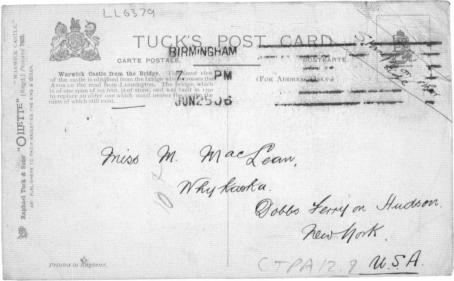

Warwick Castle postcard. These would be similar to the postcards purchased
by Mark Twain to commemorate his visit there. Raphael Tuck & Sons, 1903.

TOPO-CHICO HOT SPRINGS

MONTEREY, MEXICO

2115

Postcard mailed in the United States (despite scene) to Robert Boles, 1910.

Topo Chico hot springs, Monterey, Mexico. "Souvenir Post Card." Mailed 1907.

itinerary of going to certain places and, once there, doing certain things. While some adventurous tourists set out to explore lesser-known destinations (that is, areas not as well known by Americans or Europeans), by and large, tourism was about going somewhere, showing that you went there, and having proof of the experience. For nineteenth- and twentieth-century tourists, postcards were ideally suited for this.

The opportunity to send such cards home to friends and family presented itself well before tourists ever technically arrived at their destinations. From railroads to ocean passenger liners, postcards were readily available to tourists who wanted to communicate with others while in transit. For example, a commercially printed postcard that I pulled from my great-grandfather Robert Boles's personal collection, dated November 12, 1922, was titled "A Trip through the Orange Groves of Southern California." The postcard depicted a train traveling along tracks cutting through the citrus orchards. The back read, "Friend Bob. Waiting patiently to hear from you hope you haven't forgotten me so soon. How is Walnut Creek and everyone? L.M.B." In my family's postcards, I also came across a colorized postcard of the Topo-Chico Hot Springs, dated to June 14, 1907, and mailed from Mexico to "Mr. Nat Viara" in San Antonio, Texas. The postcard featured a donkey-driven coach that ran along Mexico's railroad line out of Monterrey in the state of Nuevo Leon. The coach is clearly taking its three tourists to the Topo-Chico hot springs and the sender scrawled "All on board, fast trx" on the front.

Because sending postcards during a journey was a rather one-sided means of communication—there was little to no expectation that the recipient would send a message back—postcards were ideally suited communiqués for people on the move. There was an asymmetry and an implicit delay in a tourist's communication via postcard.[7]

In these transit-related missives, there are two elements relevant to the overall story of postcards. The first was that the mode of transportation was worthy of a postcard image—be it a donkey-drawn railcar or southern California steam engine. As travel for tourism became more and more part of the early twentieth-century experience, it would make sense that the modes of transportation on which tourists traveled would feature on the postcards of the trips.

The second element is that the postcard isn't just being sent from the destination. Quite the contrary, in fact. These postcards were being sent en route as part of the social performance of taking a trip. It's the social equivalent of Instagramming your suitcase as you pack for a trip or posting a story with a map laid out on a table with tickets next to it, or a picture of clouds taken through an airplane window. In the performance of tourism through postcards and Instagram, you have to let people know that the trip has begun. And what better way to send that message than with a picture?

....

When postcards were at their most popular at the turn of the twentieth century, passenger liners played a major role in facilitating the physical transportation of mail as well as transporting the tourists doing the mailing. From the late nineteenth century to the middle of the twentieth, passenger liners were how millions of people moved across the world, whether they were emigrants and colonizers or tourists and soldiers. (In the 1880s, for example, historians estimate that some 650,000 people a year crossed the Atlantic to come to America—nearly 90 percent of them from northern Europe and Scandinavia.) Some passenger liners— from the Royal Mail's first full-time cruise ship, *Solent*, in 1905 to its white-hulled *Atlantis* in the 1930s—carried both postcards and people, serving as modes of transportation twice over.

Indeed, passenger liners quickly honed a niche genre of postcards that specifically catered to people in transit, tourists or otherwise. Although emigration was a major factor in accounting for the number of people who traversed the Atlantic during this period, it's the mass scale of tourism that passenger liners offered that created a new reason for people to endure a long sea voyage. And postcards were there to be bought, stamped, and sent every step of the journey.

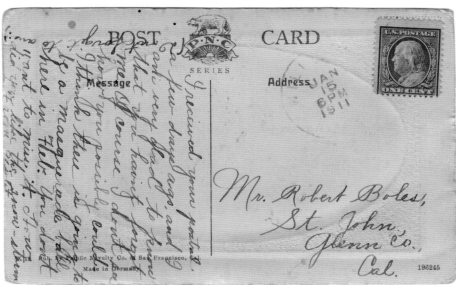

Shasta Springs postcard to Robert Boles.
Pebbled texture and stamped photograph. Mailed 1911.

"IN THE PHILIPPINES". Pacific Mail S. S. Manchuria in Manila Bay.

Photo Copyrighted by Burr Mc Intosh.

Postcard of SS *Manchuria* "in Manila Bay." Postcard printed in 1905.
The *Manchuria* was a cargo and passenger liner launched in 1903
for the Pacific Mail Steamships' trans-Pacific service.

Tourist cruise lines began to develop at the turn of the century and by the 1920s going on a cruise—as a primary act of tourism—was de rigueur for many Western tourists. (Think *Death on the Nile* by Agatha Christie, where Hercule Poirot solves a murder while aboard a steamer that takes its passengers up the Nile river. It's transit, it's tourism, but above all, it's *très chic*.) Trips aboard passenger liners took three forms: They were either one-way, round-trip, or via a route that would eventually bring the passengers back to the port from which they had left. "Passengers were treated royally at their ports of call," historian Christopher Deakes notes in his history of passenger liner postcards; "the impact of mass tourism [in the early twentieth century] was yet to be felt."[8]

But this begs two questions: What sort of postcards did passenger liners offer their tourists? And what sort of messages did tourists write on the cards? "In an age when outlets for selling a product through advertising were limited, the poster and the trade card (later, the postcard) were valuable methods of publicity, and shipowners were happy to use them," Deakes offers. "These cards were either published for shipping lines themselves, or commercially by picture postcard publishers keen to help satisfy the public's interest in ships."[9]

Early passenger liner postcards—particularly those from the 1890s— were generally produced in Germany with vibrant colors, printed lithographically on smooth cardstock. Some of these early ship-based postcards featured greetings from various German ports and often featured the ships themselves as the main focus. Centering the image on the ship invokes a sense of wonder and adventure—it leaves the implied journey well within the viewer's imagination. But it was also a way to call attention to the technological spectacle and industrial prowess that would have been associated with designing, building, and sailing such ships around the globe. These ships, the postcard images seemed to imply, were giant floating steel sculptures taking people to destinations all over the world. ("The ocean is never clear of boats of tourists," *The Sphere*, a British newspaper, groused in 1927.) By the 1930s more and more tourist cruise lines were being established in all watery nooks of the world, halted only by the advent of the Second World War. From the earliest days of cruising in the 1880s, however, passenger liners took their postcards most seriously.

Over the next decades, postcard images evolved and changed to keep pace with different art movements and general tastes. Postcards with prints of watercolor paintings, for example, became much less common as images of ships done in Art Deco or Art Nouveau styles began to take over. (And, of course, there were any number of real picture postcards of ships in dock taken by anyone with the camera and cardstock to take the image and print it out. In the real picture postcards of the Mexican Revolution, for example, the photographers aboard the uss *New Jersey* snapped some postcards while the landing battalion was docked at Veracruz, Mexico, on April 30, 1914. While one postcard is labeled "Embarking on tug for transfer to ship," it implies that the American military had been in Veracruz for a holiday of sorts, and the ship's photographers were documenting this through the recognizable touristy trope of shooting a picture of the *New Jersey* in dock.[10]) These images were ways of advertising—the ocean liners and companies, of course, but also the person sending the postcard.

It turns out that messages on ocean liner postcards were both surprising and predictable. For ships that went to warmer climates, complaining and commenting on weather filled the backs of a good many postcards. (*A Postcard History of the Passenger Liner* is full of examples of the everyday minutiae that passengers wrote on their postcards. "Starting to get roasted once more," a man wrote from Suez to a girl back home. "Had it very hot in the Red Sea," one "Harry" scrawled on the back of a postcard to a "Miss Sarah Emmerson." "It is awful hot here. One is simply pouring sweat all day and night. I sleep up on deck with nothing but pyjamas," a passenger complained.) As some of the ocean liners ran for several weeks between ports, passengers would often become preoccupied with others on the ship and postcards back home would be full of gossip of details from life on board. ("The Löwenthals seem to have missed the boat, thank goodness," Betty wrote from a Royal Mail liner approaching Lisbon. "Captain W is on board, one of the heroes of Spion Kp, he was badly wounded in the arm. Had quite a concert last night," wrote one passenger aboard a Bibby liner in 1903. "We have nice people on board and great fun with football, cricket, dancing, etc etc," Clare informed Alice as she dashed off a postcard aboard the *Ingeli* off the coast of West Africa.[11]) In short, just about every message about the experience of being "in transit" was thought up, written down, and mailed off—all on the backs of postcards. From passenger ocean liners to railroad cars to donkey-driven coaches, part of being a tourist, it would seem, is telling others about the experience.

For contemporary cruise-goers who might be charmed by the idea of mailing a postcard from their cruise, a 2020 *USA Today* Travel Tips piece walks readers through the necessary steps. "A cruise to the Bahamas

Color postcard of RMS *Carpathia*, c. 1912.
Postcards of ocean liners often served as tourist advertising.

RMS *Olympic* ocean liner postcard, c. 1910–15, Detroit Publishing Co.
The *Olympic* was the lead ship of the White Star Line, which also
included the *Titanic* and *Britannic*.

"Photochromatic" postcard showing passengers disembarking
from a ship, Algiers, Algeria, 1899.

Merchant Wharf in Shanghai, issued 1901–7.

is a relaxing tropical getaway—but even if you are on the most luxurious vacation you've ever experienced, you still might miss family and friends. Alternately, you may just want to make them a wee bit jealous," it cheerfully reports. "Whatever the reason, sending a postcard during your cruise is a good way to let your loved ones know you are thinking of them."[12] It's clear that for over seven decades, passengers traveling aboard ocean liners diligently carried out this task. But what's noteworthy about these postcards is that they were sent without the expectation that the recipient would respond to the message itself. The important thing about sending the postcards . . . is sending the postcards.

Postcards—within a few years of their invention—were quick to become social placeholders for communicating to the recipient that the sender was obeying the mores and norms of tourism. It's easy to think of postcards as simply kitschy souvenirs—the sort of things that simply have an address, a stamp, and a scribbled line something like, "Having a wonderful time, wish you were here." But postcards are the material things that connect people with geographies and geographies with people.

. . . .

So, tourists sent postcards while they embarked upon their trips. What happened when tourists got to where they were going? What sorts of postcards did they send?

During the early twentieth century, tourists—particularly American tourists—began to visit more and more places domestically and internationally, and they spent more and more money to do it. While networks of infrastructure like inns and rest stops have long been part of the experience of travel—as evidenced in the cuneiform tablets from ancient Babylonia—travel at this time was transitioning into tourism, a new leisure activity. This transformation "required infrastructure, including transportation networks, lodgings, and restaurants, as well as changes in work schedules, [that] allowed new segments of the middle and working classes to take vacations," historian Allison Marsh points out. "Destinations frequently included historic sites, spas, mountain or seaside resorts, and natural attractions, such as Niagara Falls."[13] These specific places quickly became part of a commodified landscape—images of which tourists sent back home on postcards.

The social performance of tourism is nothing new. Early on in E. M. Forster's 1908 novel *A Room with a View*, one of the main characters, Lucy Honeychurch, finds herself without a guidebook. (Specifically, in Chapter Two: "In Santa Croce with No Baedeker.") The Baedeker acted as a trusted, proper, and scripted way to be a tourist, and Lucy is lost without it. Ever since Baedeker's beginnings in the late 1820s, the publisher has offered a plethora of guides describing everything from maps and tours to views of nature and local architectures. Guidebooks eventually included Russia, Palestine, Egypt, India, and the United States, to say nothing of Europe.

A contemporary of the early 1900s Baedeker was quite forthright about their approach. In the introduction to *A Handbook for Travellers on the Continent: Being a Guide to Holland, Belgium, Prussia, Northern Germany, and the Rhine from Holland to Switzerland*, the author states, "The writer of [this] Handbook has endeavoured to confine himself to matter-of-fact descriptions of what *ought to be seen* at each place, and is calculated to interest an intelligent English traveler, without bewildering his readers with an account of all that *may* be seen."[14] To be fair, this inflexibility was imagined to be what readers were looking for—and perhaps they were—as the guidebooks of the time found their earlier counterparts to be "either general descriptions compiled by persons not acquainted with the spots" or "local histories . . . who did not sufficiently discriminate between what is peculiar to the place, and what is not worth seeing."[15]

The guidebook, then, was an important part of the infrastructure of mass tourism in no small part because it scripted out the experience for people. I like to imagine what postcards Lucy Honeychurch would have sent to her mother and brother back home in the English countryside. Fields? Flowers? The basilica at Santa Croce? If we were to follow her

"Photochrom" postcard of the Cliffs of Moher in County Clare, Ireland,
showing cliffside table and refreshments. Detroit Publishing Co., *c.* 1890–1900.

"Photochromatic" postcard from swing bridge,
Port Militaire, Brest, France, printed 1890–1905.

Baedeker guidebook, Berlin, 1910 edition. Guidebooks like the Baedeker series offered tourists proscriptive, performative itineraries for how to travel and what to see.

transition between exploring with and without the Baedeker, it would perhaps be akin to sending commercially printed postcards that featured predictable churches and other architecture—and then the turn to real picture postcards, where the point of view was singular, individual, and celebrated for being authentic. Many guidebooks pointed the reader to postcard motifs—certain landscapes, specific buildings—that would be expected of them to send home, or simply to collect for themselves.

The hundreds of millions of postcards that were produced, sold, purchased, mailed, and collected from the end of the nineteenth through the mid-twentieth century are how travelers showed to others back home that they were being "proper tourists" as well as solidifying how others perceived a place that wasn't local to them. "Tourist manuals invited readers to look at landscapes, at specified buildings or ruins, and to see places through the eyes of famous writers . . . nineteenth-century tourism was often about the commodification of specific panoramas, built environments, and literary reference points as mediated through texts," historian Eric G. E. Zeulow suggests in his history of tourism.[16]

By sending images of their travels, tourists were, in effect, creating a sort of place-based propaganda.

In going through family collections from great-grandmother Mary Virginia Stuart—Robert Boles's wife—I found several postcards from Monterrey, Mexico, that were dated between 1906 and 1910. In the late 1880s my great-great grandfather Leon Noel Stuart and his business partner Joseph Andrew Robertson moved to Monterrey from Missouri to create the first orchards of grafted orange trees in the nearby town of Montemorelos. (Robertson was also involved in a plethora of business ventures that ranged from establishing the *Monterrey News*, founding a red-brick factory, and becoming the general manager of the fledgling Monterrey & Mexican Gulf Railroad.) As a child, Mary Virginia divided her time between Redlands, California, and Monterrey. Friends and family passed through Mexico and the collection of Mexico-based postcards reflected what visitors thought Mexico ought to look like or how they ought to experience the country. The Stuarts' postcards between the United States and Mexico from the turn of the twentieth century until the beginning of Mexican Revolution also coincided with the zenith of the global postcard extravaganza. [17]

Postcards from the Stuarts' time in Mexico at the turn of the twentieth century show images of the imposing limestone formation La Huesteca around the region. There were images of factories, the city, queues of people waiting to go to work. Some featured cathedrals, casinos, hotels, and buildings. Other postcards showed halcyon, bucolic landscapes with ritzy houses nestled into the hills around the city proper. Mexican locals were invariably dressed in sombreros, either posed almost as inanimate objects (women in traditional cotton dresses, for example) or photographed farming the land. All of the postcards seemed to say either explicitly or implicitly, "Come visit Monterrey!" or "See! This is life in Monterrey!"

But these postcards are also completely predictable and interchangeable—without knowing that the postcards are from Mexico, it would be completely possible to think that they're from just about anywhere.

Without the label of "Robles Church, Monterrey, Mexico" it is very difficult for a viewer to know what church they are looking at and where. The
different images—the tropes, the genres, the physical framing—aren't
unique to postcards from Mexico. They're the same tropes, genres, and
framing that sold postcards the world over; creating expectations for
how postcards ought to look, yes, but also how visitors expected the
cities and people to be, based on the images that were sold on postcards.

One of the postcards in the family collection was addressed to
"Miss Virginia Stewart" at "Matemorelos, Nueva Leon, Mexico." (Yes,
her last name was misspelled.) The front offers a market scene with
several seated women selling vegetables and several children standing
in the background. Two of the seated women seem to be looking at the
photographer straight on, while the other is looking off to her left. Three
lean-to shade umbrellas are propped up on the cobblestone streets. The
scene is titled, "A Street Market, Guadalajara, Mexico. Sonora News
Company, City of Mexico. Photo by Scott."

The colorized photograph is one of a series that the Sonora News
Co. printed and sold—there's a serial number, 2873, above the caption—and the idea was that these postcards were meant to capture
everyday life in Mexico. (At least, a version of "everyday life" that would
appeal to tourists buying postcards.) The stamp shows that the card was
posted in the 10 a.m. mail on May 31, 1908. The back of the postcard
was printed in large green letters, "República Mexicana Tarjeta Postal"
with a smaller printed line beneath it that said, "This Space May Be
Used for Correspondence."

Arrived here right side up with care. Have not been able to
get any postcards before. Am not working yet. Expect to go to
New York by way of Monterrey in Sept. Would like to stop if
you are still at home then but cannot make it any sooner. This
is a nice town, (for Mexico). Let me hear from you again in the
near future. Sincerely, your friend, Vassar Soule

Postcard of Cairo showing the Pyramids of Giza, unknown date.

Postcard of Thebes showing Temple Deir el-Bahri, unknown date.

Sonora News Company, Casino in Monterrey, Mexico. Mailed 1906.
There is no space allocated for a message, just the addressee and address.

Other postcards from the family collection from Mexico—cards that were sent to family members during various trips—include several colorized lithograph postcards, from the Sonora News Co. again, with everyday scenes from Monterrey. In reading through the different postcards, one of the things that struck me were the phrases that the writer used to argue for the authenticity of the scene—implicitly arguing that their experience in Monterrey was all the more authentic because they themselves had seen what the postcard depicted.

For example, there was a postcard of the Hotel Marmol from Topo Chico in Monterrey—the same Topo Chico, as it happens, with the donkey-drawn railcar that took tourists to and from the location, since it was a little bit outside the city proper. The postcard shows a clean, tree-lined street with a pastoral view of grasses and flowers and mountains in the distance, a view that guests would have had from the hotel windows. ("A very pretty place. Helen 2/25/06," the postcard reads.) Interpreting the postcard as a social connection between Helen and Virginia, it is clear that Helen is signaling that she has been there and is personally vouching for the authenticity of idyllic scene.

Another Sonora News Co. postcard shows a horse-drawn streetcar and a man walking along with a bicycle. The city street, with the white, three-story building behind it, could be just about anywhere, but the label clarifies that it is "Casino—Monterrey, Mexico." The back of the "Tarjeta Postal" is only for the recipient's address ("Lado que se reserve para la dirección") and was stamped as arriving in Brooklyn to Miss Alice M. Cogsurill/Cogswill on February 27, 1906. Since the back of the card didn't have room for a message, the sender scrunched a penciled note on the front underneath the photo. ("2-23-06. There should be or there is another donkey in front of the one you see for the st. car tandem ride.")

Again, the sender offers a commentary on how the scene "ought" to look—it needed the second donkey for the viewer to see how the streetcars "really" functioned in Monterrey—and the postcard was a chance for him to validate the authenticity of the image on the postcards because he was seeing the image acted out in real life. Travelers—like those visiting Monterrey—were able to show that they were proper tourists by sending postcards, thus vouching for the authenticity of areas they were visiting. Taken all together, these postcards managed to capture an ethos of tourism at the turn of the twentieth-century Monterrey, Mexico—at least a sense of life in Monterrey that postcard manufacturers would have thought appealed to postcard purchasers.

....

However, as was the case with many of the postcards marketed to tourists, it is impossible to get away from the question of who photographed the subjects and landscapes, the power dynamics between the subject and photographer, and the photographers' expectations and intentions for the visual message of their postcard image. In other words, like the real picture postcards that Walter Horne shot of the Mexican Revolution, many of the postcards from this time catered to tourists' preconceptions about the peoples and places that they were visiting.

Images on postcards became a way of demonstrating to others that you, as a tourist, had participated in the power structure that essentially turned local peoples into landscapes—something to be seen, checked off, and commodified. Sending postcards like this—particularly postcards of "exotic" non-Westerners—turned people into spectacle and relegated them to part of the backdrop and a tourist experience. If you add a layer of colonialism and empire on top of the tourism, it's little wonder that postcards invariably distanced the buyer and sender from those pictured. They were "those people"—the Other. Postcards have an implicit power of gaze and perspective.

This "Us" and "Other" dynamic is particularly apparent in colonial-era postcards that were made, sent, and received during the first half of the twentieth century. The 2018 exhibition *World on the Horizon* (curated by art historian Prita Meier at the Smithsonian's National Museum of African Art) highlighted just how British colonial geographies in Kenya, Tanzania, and Somalia were made and remade between the 1890s and the 1920s through colonially produced material culture, especially picture

Front of Hotel Marmol, Topo Chico. Unmailed, c. 1910s.

postcards. Early East African photography, Meier explained in an NPR interview, "show[s] the compelling and amazing ways that people living on the Swahili coast quickly embraced photography, especially portraits, and made the art their own."[18] In these images, men and women from the Swahili coast are shown in a variety of portrait poses, as portraiture was a popular, inexpensive pastime in the three decades around the turn of the twentieth century.

But colonial postcards—particularly those from *World on the Horizon*—have a particularly "problematic history," as Meier notes. The postcards in this series were created without the subjects' permission or knowledge, and were produced specifically for European and American audiences. After taking pictures, the portrait photographer would order thousands of postcards from a single negative. "The postcards would be sold throughout the West and also be sent back to coastal towns in Africa, where they were marketed to Western tourists, who would mail

Studio portrait of Ani Chokyi, taken at Thomas Paar studio in 1890s and turned into a color postcard around 1900 specifically to appeal to British tourists in Darjeeling.

Women weaving carpets, Algiers, Algeria, 1899. Often crafts, arts, and peoples were objectified through a photographer's lens to create postcards that would appeal to tourists looking to see the visited place as "Other."

the cards back home," journalist Melody Schreiber outlines in her review of the exhibition for NPR. The images would travel the world several times over, all without the knowledge or consent of those photographed. ("Can you imagine a private family photograph being turned into a tourist souvenir?" Meier points out.[19]) Although *World on the Horizon* focused on the exploitation of those photographed, it also highlighted how the peoples of the Swahili coast made and remade certain elements of Western culture—fabrics, fashions, and the like.

East Africa wasn't the only source of British colonial picture post-cards. *From Madras to Bangalore: Picture Postcards as Urban History of Colonial India*, held at SOAS University of London in 2018, emphasized how picture postcards were used by British citizens living in India to send home images of what life in India was "really like." (This isn't unlike the tourist postcards that implicitly vouched for the postcard image's authenticity by adding, supplementing, or narrating the picture that was being mailed.) The exhibition showcased three hundred picture postcards that had been mailed to Europe from India between 1900 and the 1930s. "We don't want the postcards to be a vehicle of colonial nostalgia. It is the opposite of that," Stephen Putnam Hughes, a co-curator with Emily Rose Stevenson explained to the BBC. "We wanted to provide enough evidence from the colonial past and allow people to look at the images critically."[20]

The exhibition focused on postcards from Chennai (formerly Madras) and Bangalore and carefully walked audiences through the different power dynamics and racism that were being played out in the different picture postcards. There were images of Indian men preparing a bath for Europeans and Indian women working as washerwomen. These sorts of picture postcards of Indians in subservient roles were a way for the Europeans living in India to elevate their status among those receiving the postcards back home. "Postcards certainly reinforced European stereotypes of Indians and contributed to the construction of fixed, defined characteristics of particular groups," Hughes offered to the BBC.[21]

The perspectives, gazes, and subjects might have varied across the decades and over six continents as more and more of the middle and working classes around the world sent and received billions of postcards. But this material social network depended on tourists knowing that part of being a proper tourist, or a proper traveler, was sending postcards back home.

. . . .

As I was writing this chapter, my grandmother happened to send me three postcards that she had bought while she and my grandfather were on vacation in France in 1990. There were two postcards from the famous Paleolithic cave at Lascaux that featured images of iconic cave paintings from 17,000 years ago, and one of Notre-Dame cathedral in Paris. The cards arrived in an envelope with a bright yellow Post-it note stuck to the first one that read, "Ran into these—might be of interest to you for your book. Love, Grandma. P.S. We've been there."

On the one hand, they were simply three postcards that "authenticated" my grandparents' trip to France. ("We've been there.") Interestingly, however, in the decades since my grandparents bought and saved the postcards, they've come to mark particular moments in France's history—particularly, how tourists see and experience the country. On the other hand, these three postcards mark time as well as geography, because what one sees on the postcards isn't what a contemporary tourist would see if they were to visit today. When the Paleolithic site Lascaux opened to the public on July 14, 1948, visitors could walk through the cave to see the hundreds of paintings that featured large megafauna such as bulls and elk as well as human-like figures and abstract shapes. But by 1955 the effects of hundreds of thousands of tourists had begun to take a toll on the Paleolithic art. Lichens and molds began to grow on the walls, destroying the paintings, and Lascaux was closed to tourists in 1963 in an effort to save the art. Today visitors can "see" Lascaux's Paleolithic paintings thanks to replicas of the site that are nearby.

Postcard of the "Rajah Rest House" published by S. M. Manicum,
a firm from Penang, now Malaysia. Issued c. 1910–19.

"Afrique Occidentale (Sénégal) Dakar Hôtel de Ville," 1920.

Replica or not, Lascaux is still an iconic tourist destination. ("You saw the Eiffel Tower, the Seine, the Louvre. Wait, you didn't see Lascaux?!? Really!?") "Lascaux has often been referred to as the prehistoric equivalent of the Sistine Chapel and it's a fitting comparison," *Lonely Planet France* instructs readers.[22] Buying, sending, and collecting postcards from Lascaux is part of being a proper tourist to the Dordogne region of France.

When my grandparents visited Lascaux and bought postcards, they were visiting the replica, but the images on the postcards are from Lascaux itself. The photos are printed on a linen-like cardstock—the card's fibers show through the thick ink and when I run my finger over the card, I can feel tiny ridges. The backs of the cards are divided, with space on the right for the recipient's address and the left side labeled as "Grotte de Lascaux (Dordogne)" and "Grotte de Lascaux—Dordogne 'Chapelle Sixtine de la Préhistoire'." Enough space was left for a short message should the purchaser wish to send the cards. (These Paleolithic paintings, as the postcard explained, were the "Sistine Chapel of Prehistory.") The Lascaux postcards were in good condition three decades after their purchase in France. The corners were a bit rounded and the inner cardstock a bit exposed, but it was clear that my grandmother had carefully kept them as mementos of the trip.

The third of my grandparents' postcards from France showed Notre-Dame cathedral at night. ("Paris, Notre-Dame illuminée" read the back of the postcard. "Collectionnez les Cartes Postales!") Using the cars parked off to the side of the building as a rough estimate, it looks as if the picture of Notre-Dame was taken some time in the late 1980s. The finish on the postcard is glossy and, like the postcards from Lascaux, the card's corners were slightly rounded with wear.

I can't imagine how many times the cathedral had been bought, messaged, sent, and collected via tourists' postcards over the course of the last 150 years, and my grandparents were no exception. But on April 15, 2019, a structural fire broke out beneath the roof of the cathedral, destroying the building's spire and most of the wooden roof. Images of the fire flooded the Internet and the world mourned. France's president, Emmanuel Macron, has vowed that the iconic cathedral will be restored and rebuilt.[23] Regardless, the Notre-Dame that the world and its tourists now have is—and will be, when rebuilt—very different from the Notre-Dame on my grandmother's postcard from 1990. Twenty-first century postcards (and their digital equivalent, Instagram posts) will be able to be "dated" based on the fire. Just as I was able to offer a guess as to when the postcard for my grandparents' trip in 1990 was taken based on the cars, the Notre-Dame fire and its architectural aftermath will offer a way to historically mark when that person took the image.

These sorts of subtle cues about different Notre-Dame postcards help to mark different historical moments of tourists looking at and buying images of the cathedral. The place might be the same, but how it is commemorated is as much about the moment of commemoration as it is about the monument itself. Postcards might be a mass medium, and we might talk about them as they number in the hundreds of billions, but postcards can still mark a specific historical moment—and in the case of Notre-Dame, a historical point that we can't go back to. The cathedral's steeple that features so prominently in my grandparents' postcard, for example, no longer stands.

. . . .

Does being a tourist in the twenty-first century still require sending postcards? Has Instagram simply taken over that performative niche? Yes and no.

"Until a few years ago, hardly a day would go by in the summer without the mailman bringing a postcard from a vacationing friend or acquaintance," contemporary Serbian American poet Charles Simic suggested in a 2011 op-ed in *The Guardian* lamenting the lost art of postcard sending. "It wasn't just the Eiffel Tower or the Taj Mahal or some other famous tourist attraction you were likely to receive in the mail, but also a card with a picture of a roadside diner in Iowa, the biggest hog at some state fair in the south, or even a funeral parlour touting the professional excellence that their customers have come to expect over a hundred years."[24]

It's impossible to separate postcards from tourism, and the twenty-first century has found some unique ways to offer new life to postcards and reinforce—reinvent, perhaps—a social network built out of images printed on cardstock and mailed around the world by tourists. For example, rather than take for granted that tourists will send postcards of their own accord, the Postal Museum in London has postcards for sale in the museum's gift shop, a machine that prints postage (international postage, even), a table with tethered pens to fill out the purchased cards, and a conveniently located red mailbox to put them in once you have written and addressed them. The Postal Museum is catering to the activity of sending a postcard that naturally coincides with a trip to a museum—I saw one kid pose for a photograph before dramatically dropping his postcard in the mailbox. I sent postcards from the Postal Museum while in London, several, in fact. I felt that they were a tasteful counterpart to the fantastically kitschy Britannia-themed ones I had found and mailed to my sister's kids several days prior.

Another uniquely twenty-first-century chapter of postcard history comes from Timbuktu in Mali. Where Timbuktu was once an exotic, legendary destination for the most ardently adventurous tourists, a reputation built in no small part through decades of breathless travel literature, the geopolitics of the twenty-first century have not been particularly kind to the tourism industry and over the last decade, tourism in Timbuktu has ground to a halt. (On April 9, 2019, the U.S. State Department re-upped its travel advisory for Americans thinking about going to Mali. "Do not travel to Mali due to crime, terrorism, and kidnapping. Threat Level 4: Do Not Travel. If you do decide to travel to Mali, draft a will, and designate appropriate insurance beneficiaries and/or power of attorney."[25]) But you can still send and receive postcards from Timbuktu without having to actually go there.

The project, Postcards from Timbuktu, was established in 2016 by Phil Paoletta, an American hotel owner from Cleveland, and Ali Nialy, a 29-year-old guide from Timbuktu, and the idea was that the project would help create some income for tourist guides. In 2016 Paoletta was living in Bamako, the capital of Mali, which is about 600 miles from Timbuktu, running a hotel that catered to UN envoys and NGOs. Paoletta wanted to do something for Timbuktu to bridge the gap left by tourists. ("Nialy and other guides accept that tourists likely won't come back for a long time, given the ongoing insecurity."[26]) He began to experiment with how long it would take to send a postcard from Timbuktu to the United States and Europe. It took a couple of weeks, but the postcards arrived.

Postcards from Timbuktu invites "digital tourists" to browse through the website's twelve different postcard options—some contemporary, some decidedly invoking earlier postcards from the early 1900s—and pick a postcard that they want Nialy's team of postcard writers in Timbuktu to pen and put in the post. Postcards can be sent anywhere that has a reliable postal service with an address that is provided by the purchaser and postcard messages have been written in Italian, French, English, Swedish, Dutch, German, and Arabic. ("While we have found the Post Office of Mali to be reliable, it is not particularly swift," the website's FAQ section points out.[27]) It can take up to four weeks for the postcard to arrive after purchase and the website reminds people to be patient.

Although Timbuktu has a functioning mail service, getting postcards to and from the city is no small feat. The effort required to trek the postcards from Timbuktu to Bamako is far from insignificant and the price factors in the transportation costs; a postcard is currently priced at U.S.$10, which includes the card and international postage. But, and this is key to Postcards from Timbuktu being a twenty-first century phenomenon, updates are posted to Instagram for followers to track. "A new batch of postcards has just arrived from #Timbuktu. Now the second part of their journey begins. They've already been on 3 different motorbikes and a plane," @postcardsfromtimbuktu's Instagram account announced in a post.[28]

Front of contemporary postcard from Timbuktu,
showing wear and tear of journey, 2018.

Posting updates like these becomes a way to act out the authenticity of the postcards coming all the way from Timbuktu. (I've sent friends and relatives postcards from there.) Postcards from Timbuktu and gift shops like that of the Postal Museum have fully and explicitly embraced the performance of postcard sending in a way that is unique to the twenty-first century. No longer only a subtle act of validation and authentication of a trip or experience as a tourist, sending contemporary postcards has become a performance all on its own—one that doesn't necessarily depend on physically going to a place and then telling friends and family that you were there.

. . . .

Not long after my grandmother sent me the postcards from France, I spent a weekend in Galveston, Texas, and picked up several postcards at a gas station to send to members of my extended family. Postcards have been so completely ingrained in how I think about travel that I couldn't be a tourist somewhere and not send a postcard from the trip.

I put one in the mail for my grandmother, the one who had sent along the old postcards from her trip to France. The postcard selection at the gas station was a bit limited but I found one with a sunset over the Gulf of Mexico and "Galveston" spelled out in iconic cursive script. I wrote something like, "The beach is beautiful!" before dropping the card in a blue mailbox outside my hotel. I had, to use her words, "been there."

FIVE

POSTCARDS FROM COUNTRIES THAT NO LONGER EXIST

....

Aden. Basutoland. Bavaria. Benadir. Biafra. Cape Juby. Ciskei. Corrientes. Czechoslovakia. Hajez. Hatay. Hawaii. The Holy Roman Empire. The Irish Free State. Khairpur. The Kingdom of the Two Sicilies. Kraków. Ligurian Republic. Louenço Marques. Mafeking. The Mali Federation. Montenegro. Nejd. Orange Free State. Rhodesia. Siberia. South Russia. Tannu Tuva. The USSR. Van Diemen's Land. Vichy France. The West Indies Federation. The Yemen Arab Republic. Yugoslavia. Zaire. Zanzibar.

Acre. Bohemia and Moravia. The Confederation of Peru and Bolivia. Denmark-Norway. The District of Assiniboia. The Falkland Islands Dependencies. Gold Coast. Gwalior. His Majesty's Settlements in the Bay of Honduras. Jhalawar. Kiauchau. Modena. Persia. Prince Edward Island. Republic of Geneva. Republic of Valais. Rio de la Plata. Saarland. Sandur. Tobago. Trinidad. Ubangi-Shari (Central African Empire.) Waziristan. The Zoutpansberg Republic.

Abyssinia. Allenstein. Alwar. Boyaca. Carnaro and Fiume. The Danish West Indies. The Duchy of Parma and Piacenza. Eastern Karelia. Eastern Rumelia. Elobey, Annobon and Corisco. The Far Eastern Republic. Inini. Iquique. The Iraqi-Saudi Arabian Neutral Zone. Kiaochow. Manchukuo. Muscat and Oman. Nandgaon. Saseno.

South Kasai. South Shetland Islands. The Tangier International Zone. The Canal Zone. The Channel Islands. The South Moluccas. Tierra del Fuego. Tripolitania. Vancouver Island. Zululand.

Some of these names might be familiar, some maybe not. Spread out over six continents and two hundred years, they have one thing in common: Today, they are all dead countries.

. . . .

"In better philatelic circles a dead country is the term used for a place, not necessarily a sovereign country, that once issued postage stamps but now longer does so, usually because it has ceased to exist," writer and stamp collector Les Harding explains in *Dead Countries of the Nineteenth and Twentieth Centuries*. "Although I do collect stamps, my interest in dead countries has probably arisen from the fact that I was born in a dead country—Newfoundland."[1]

Countries change. History is nothing if not full of shifting borders, emerging geopolitical entities, and the rise and collapse of nation-states. Here, in the twenty-first century, it's easy to think of dead countries as simply relics of historical geography. (Like finding Siam on an old *Risk* gameboard, for example.) But the making and remaking of countries is very much a part of current geopolitics. Socio-political upheaval and change cannot simply be ascribed to colonialism and the empire-building of earlier centuries.

Contemporary countries and their borders are ever-changing. East Timor, Kosovo, and South Sudan, for example, number among the world's youngest countries, recognized in 2002, 2008, and 2011, respectively. Jammu and Kashmir have experienced a sixty-year border dispute between Pakistan, India, and China about what territory belongs to which country. Yugoslavia broke up in 1992 and the (smaller) Federal Republic of Yugoslavia was itself terminated in 2003. The country of Serbia and Montenegro had a short three-year run from 2003 to 2006 before the two regions declared their independence from each other. And the Autonomous Republic of Crimea was annexed by the Russian

Postcard to Riga, Latvia (Russian Empire), 1873. The instructions on the bottom
of the postcard note that it is an "open letter" and that the postage must be paid in full.
This early style of postcard does not have a picture illustration.

Federation in 2014. (Today, Russia administers Crimea and the federal city of Sevastopol as federal subjects of the Russian Federation; however, Ukraine, most international governments, and the UN General Assembly Resolution consider Crimea part of Ukraine.) Countries are not static and never have been.

This begs the question, then, of what makes a country a country. "The concept is old, but also notoriously slippery," British geographer Nick Middleton offers in *An Atlas of Countries That Don't Exist*. "As soon as you set out to find a clear definition you start running into discrepancies, exceptions and anomalies."[2] The more we try to pin down a definition, the more complicated the question becomes. Is a country made by demarcating boundaries on a map? A capital city? Language? A shared story of origin? A national narrative? A functioning bureaucracy, ensuring that the day-to-day business of the country continues to transpire? Legitimacy through global governing bodies?

If so, what would these criteria mean for countries that don't fit into these categories? Crimea, for example? Or for autonomous regions inside larger recognized states, like Lakotah in Canada, Greenland in Denmark, Catalonia in Spain, or Abkhazia or South Ossetia in Georgia? "The 'nation' proved an invention on which it was impossible to secure a patent," historian Benedict Anderson offers in his classic text *Imagined Communities*. He was describing how difficult it is to assess the concepts of "country" and "nation" in the early twentieth century as emerging countries contended with the legacy of colonialism. All autonomous regions still grapple with these issues.[3] Yet although a nation is difficult to define, its administration offers a way to understand how a national identity can be built, curated, and disseminated.

Middleton suggests that, at least for contemporary countries, membership in the General Assembly of the United Nations is good starting point, as this is the world's most significant state-based international organization. But this benchmark also becomes complicated—Israel became a member of the world body in 1949, but more than thirty other UN members do not recognize Israel's existence. Likewise, the UN recognizes countries that do not have full membership. The UN formally recognizes the state of Palestine; many of its members do not. Taiwan has full UN membership but, owing to its complicated relationship to China, does not run official embassies around the world. The United Kingdom, recognized by the UN as only one entity, is comprised of four separate countries: England, Wales, Scotland, and Northern Ireland. (Middleton points out that all four have separate sports teams for everything aside from the Olympics—a different and not insignificant arbitrator of nationhood.) Back in Sevastopol, we find that assigning Crimea to a specific country has become an overtly political act in the second decade of the twenty-first century.

But just because a country is historically "dead" doesn't mean that its peoples, cultures, and histories have gone extinct along with its geographic borders. The lives of people who live and have lived in nineteenth- and twentieth-century dead countries can be traced through material culture like postcards. (Centuries of colonial rule and its systematic efforts at indigenous erasure, for example, illustrate how peoples can be written out of national narratives and must work to reclaim a place in the history of the country itself. These are nations and confederations that have been subjugated to an imposed political rule.) Although the term "dead countries" might be best known in the stamp-collecting world, postcards from countries that don't exist anymore show us the making, unmaking, and re-making of contemporary nations.

During the nineteenth and twentieth centuries, colonial powers such as Spain, Portugal, France, the Netherlands, Russia, Turkey, and Germany found that establishing postal systems and regulating the postage and post routes within their various colonies and territories ensured a measure of control and regulation. (British Somaliland, for example, began issuing stamps that were specifically printed with its name on June 1, 1903. The Portuguese colony of Macao issued stamps on November 3, 1925.) These were the sorts of social institutions that ensured the "success" of a country or empire and have been paired with imperial expansion for millennia.

BIRRI POOL, NR. DEM-ZUBEIR

G. N. MORHIG
THE ENGLISH PHARMACY

Postcard from Britain's Anglo-Egyptian Sudan (today Sudan).
"Birri Pool, Nr. Dem-Zubeir." Published by G. N. Morhig,
The English Pharmacy, Khartoum. Mailed December 1906.

The global geopolitical turmoil at the turn of the twentieth century guaranteed that there was no shortage of wars, skirmishes, and revolutions. The British Empire was busy fighting its protracted and costly Boer War in South Africa; imperial Russia was cracking under protests from workers and students, France's interests in Africa were under threat from other colonial powers, and Germany was pursuing an incredibly uneven foreign policy. Japan became the first non-Western state to launch a program of systematic state-sponsored industrialization and, with its modern army and navy, expanded its own imperial reach to control Korea, Taiwan, and Port Arthur on the Manchurian mainland. And the United States pushed its expansionist agenda with its annexation of the Philippine Islands at the end of the Spanish-American War.

These international conflicts inevitably tested and transformed national borders and geo-political entities. But through it all, people sent each other postcards and depended on the social and national institutions necessary—like a postal system—for sending and receiving those cards. As a mass-produced medium, postcards are very good at tracking evolving national narratives and how those were sent out into the world; they're not so good at reflecting on the machinery of their own propaganda. "Countries will forever try to present themselves exactly the way they want to be seen," Bjørn Berge neatly summarizes in *Nowherelands: An Atlas of Vanished Countries, 1840–1975*.[4] Postcards—whether unique or commercially mass-produced—are an effective means of propaganda, whether it is explicit nationalism or implicit nation-building.

Consequently, postcards formed the first global social network as empires expanded, colonial rule lingered, and political revolutions saw the births and deaths of a plethora of countries. Postcards from dead countries show a complex history of social reorganization just as much as they demonstrate colonialism, empire-building, and the making of national mythologies.

....

"Picture postcards are tantalizing objects," historian Alison Rowley points out in her book *Open Letters: Russian Popular Culture and the Picture Postcard, 1880–1922*. "Produced in numbers dwarfing the print runs of poster or popular prints and available in every corner of the [Russian] empire, picture postcards had the power not only to reflect popular culture, but also to shape it."[5] Postcards mark Russia's geography and nation-building as few other artifacts can.

Early picture postcards from the Russian Empire show four tumultuous decades of Russian history that encompassed three revolutions, two world wars, and a civil war before the Union of Soviet Socialist Republics was established in 1922. Because picture postcards were not necessarily formally issued by a government, "it is possible to discern the multiplicity of the often-contradictory aptitudes, beliefs, and values swirling through popular culture at the time," Rowley contends.[6] This tracks with the myriad types of postcard that were coming into Russia as well as postcards that Russians were sending to each other and abroad.

Broadly, of course, postcards from dead countries offer snapshots of how a place is unmade and remade as national borders and geographic boundaries change. Specifically in Russia, postcards offer a historical timeline, told through a mass-produced medium, of social and political changes to countries: the expansion of the Russian Empire, the formation of the USSR, and then the creation of Russian Federation as it continues to annex regions today.

Postcards entered global circulation in force in the 1870s. The first unstamped, plain postcards began to show up in Russian post by January 1, 1872, and the production of postcards became centralized by the Russian postal authorities. In 1874 Russia was one of 22 countries that agreed to abide by international postcard regulations; these required participating countries not only to recognize the postage paid to send postcards, but to regulate the size of postcards to 9 × 14 centimeters (3½ × 5½ in.). (The dimensions of postcards have been legislated many times throughout the last century and a half and vary greatly depending on the decade and the country in question.)

Historical estimates suggest that the Universal Postal Union—which established the Treaty of Bern in 1874—handled 231.5 million postcards just one year later in 1875. By 1900 they were dealing with something like 2.8 billion postcards per year. The Russian government transferred its monopoly on postcards to the Ministry of the Interior in December 1894, and it wasn't until 1898 that the Society of St Eugenia was allowed to enter the Russian postcard market and postcard sellers from Stockholm, Paris, and Berlin began to sell postcards to eager customers, despite the particularly tumultuous social politics of the time. In February 1904, the Russian government allowed messages to be written on the backs of postcards and the first Russian cartoon postcards were published.[7]

By this time, imperial Russia was just as much part of the global postcard craze as the United States and Europe. In fact, Russia took a lot of its postcard inspiration from its European counterparts, particularly in how to manufacture postcards, what subjects, landscapes, or motifs to put on the cards, and of course, how to use them. By the 1900s it was hard to find corners of the globe that weren't somehow connected to each other through mass media. Just what sorts of postcards did mid- to late nineteenth-century Russians buy and send? The same sorts people bought and sold outside of Russia—of anything and everything.

"Greetings from" postcards were particularly popular. Landscapes. Celebrity portraits, especially of the tsar's family and other famous political leaders. (Queen Victoria had allowed portraits of the British royal family to be produced on postcards; the Russian imperial family followed suit.) Bridges, buildings, any sort of engineering achievement similar to projects that were photographed and printed as "real picture" postcards in the United States and Europe. (The famous Georgian Military Road that runs through the Caucasus Mountains has been a long-standing staple of picture postcards of the nineteenth and twentieth centuries, regardless of which nation governs it. The 1914 edition of *Baedeker's Russia with Teheran, Port Arthur, and Peking: A Handbook for Travellers*, for example, lavishes praise on it, calling it

Postcard from Copenhagen to Fellin, Levonia (Russian Empire), present-day Estonia. Mailed 1905. This style of postcard does not have a picture illustration.

"one of the most beautiful mountain roads in the world.")[8] All of the subject matter worked to create a carefully curated sense of Russian-ness that would be reinforced as the images circulated around the world. And, of course, as tourists bought and sent postcards, certain motifs became more and more ingrained in the global consciousness of "imperial Russia."

Postcards with holiday greetings for Christmas, New Year's, and Easter were enduringly popular across several decades, from the mid-1800s through the Russian Revolution, originally made with very European-looking holiday motifs. In particular, these holiday cards showed sentimentalized scenes generally featuring children; the captions in various languages were simply changed to be written in Russian. Although holiday postcards were incredibly popular with consumers

La Famille Impériale de Russie

PHOTOGRAPHIÉ A PETERHOF LE 16 AOUT 1901
PAR L. LEVITSKY
PHOTOGRAPHE DE LL. MAJESTÉS

NEURDEIN FRÈRES, ÉDITEURS

REPRODUCTION INTERDITE

Family portrait of Tsar Nicholas II taken by Sergei Levitsky,
manufactured by Neurdein Frères. Postmarked September 19, 1901.

—and, indeed, circulated for years after the public celebration of the holidays was banned after the Revolution—efforts to forcibly circulate postcards from the October Revolution simply didn't garner the same enthusiasm among Soviet citizens, despite the fact that these patriotic postcards were manufactured in huge quantities. The holiday postcards from a then newly deceased country (Russia) proved to be much more popular than the contemporary Soviet-style ones.[9]

For as long as the medium has existed, postcards have accompanied newspapers, posters, and other print media as a significant part of any empire's expansion. In Russia's case, early twentieth-century landscape postcards helped build a rhetoric that the country's government—rather than the tsar or the Orthodox Church—ought to be credited with Russia's economic development and its nation-building along what were then the frontiers of the Russian Empire. Where printed materials like maps relied, nominally, on demarcating a nation based on its geographical borders, picture postcards featuring landscape images could create an *impression* of a nation. And, of course, postcards of maps of different geopolitical divisions within Russia were popular; those that were printed with official-looking crests and coats-of-arms ("badges of territorial possession"[10]) helped craft a national narrative. "Because images reproduced on picture postcards fixed boundaries in a variety of ways, they negated the fluidity of actual borders," Rowley notes. "Through these omissions, picture postcards were instrumental in constructing imaginary geographies of the Russian Empire."[11]

Many of the images on nation-building postcards from this time period were originally photographs, whether the postcard was a real picture postcard or simply lithographed from an original photograph. As such, they offered an implicit rhetoric of truth and authenticity that reproductions of landscape watercolors or holiday-greeting postcards do not (much like the visual rhetoric of Walter Horne's postcards of the Mexican Revolution or the real photo postcards from the women's suffrage movements.) These postcards become a way of reinforcing the idea of Russian nation-building and nationalism, because photographs inspire confidence in their viewer about the "truth" of the view they offer. Picture postcards are easy artifacts to read as part of the national story of Russia.

"In the mid-twentieth century, the Soviet government issued postcards to teach schoolchildren geography in the USSR," Rowley explained to me as I interviewed her about Russian postcard history. "Sometimes these postcards were stand-ins for official textbooks. It was cheaper and easier to ensure that schoolchildren had official postcards than official textbooks."[12]

But it's a complicated story when the postcard medium reflects social anxieties and brewing national confrontations. Postcards weren't simply for the elite and bourgeoisie who could afford to travel and be tourists. They were part of an active system of anti-imperialist propaganda that ran from Siberia to Moscow, with postcards being mailed from Western Europe thanks to European sympathizers as well as Russian intelligentsia living in exile. ("In the early 1900s, the situation inside the Empire started to deteriorate," historian Tobie Mathew points out, helping to contextualize how postcards became more explicitly pressed into political propaganda. "The industrial revolution that boosted the publishing industry was also greasing the wheels of political dissent."[13]) Just as postcards were an integral part of building a national narrative of Russia, they were also part of imperial Russia's downfall.

Although official postcards were printed through state media, many were not. Rogue, anti-imperialist postcards began showing up by the 1870s. Official mail workers intercepted and censored postcards that they felt were existential or literal threats to the tsar. In the ensuing decade, postcards offered a democratizing voice and a counterpoint to the tightly controlled state media. Postcards were so commonplace and so easy to manufacture that it was impossible for a government to control all printing, or all of the postcards streaming into Russia from outside of the country, despite serious efforts to do so.

For revolutionaries, postcards could be just as much a form of social performance as they were for tourists showing off their travels.

Postcard with Christmas greetings, predating the Russian Revolution.
Holiday postcards were extremely popular in the Russian Empire prior to 1917.

"Most anti-government postcards were never sent through the post,"
Mathew explains; "they were instead passed from hand to hand or kept
for personal use."[14] Consequently, postcards were incredibly effective
vehicles of popular dissent, especially when it came to contentious pol-
icies like land reform and censorship. One example that Mathew points
to in his research about postcards of the Russian Revolution is that of
Pavel Evstifev—a sort of nineteenth-century Russian everyman—who
in 1898 sent a postcard to his local council complaining about having
to pay for grazing rights. "Why are we not given grass and forest land
for free?" Evstifev insisted. "You are rich and stuff your pockets, while
we get nothing at all."[15] This sort of interaction—critique, really—with
government officials would have been extremely difficult through other
media. Much like tweeting complaints to a governmental agency (#MTA

Postcard titled "The road, the first bridge, Groussie [Georgia], Russia."
Detroit Publishing Company, printed 1890–1900.

"Devil's Bridge," the same bridge as featured in the Photochrom postcard
on the Georgian Military Road. No manufacturer listed, n.d.

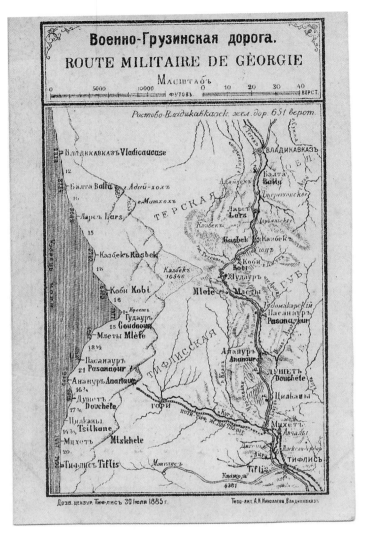

Map of the "Georgian Military Road" (a major travel route through
the Caucasus from contemporary Georgia to Russia) with mountain altitudes
included on the side. Manufactured by Tipo-lit A.N. Nikolaeva, Vladikavkaz.
Design passed by censors in 1883.

or #FixTheSubway in New York City, for example) or company (@Delta, @AmericanAirlines for customer complaints) here in the twenty-first century, a postcard was a way to send a short message across socio-economic lines. As a medium, it offered a democratizing interaction.

Social and political tensions across the empire mounted and, "as the twentieth century opened, Russia was in turmoil," historian Nicholas Risanovsky describes. "Strikes spread throughout the country. Student protests and disturbances became more frequent, constituting an almost continuous series from 1898 on."[16] Postcards followed along every bit of the political turmoil.

Then, on Sunday, January 22, 1905, postcards became part of the 1905 revolution. Soldiers from Tsar Nicolas II's Imperial Guard fired on unarmed demonstrators who were marching toward the Winter

Real picture postcard of Georgian Military Road mountain pass.
Manufactured by Scherer, Nabholz & Co., Moscow, 1902.

Au bon jardinier. – Spécialité de poires Duchesśes

Postcard caricature by G. Bigoty mocking Nicholas II's
lack of a male heir. No manufacturer or date listed.

Stamped postcard of Vladimir Lenin from the USSR, 1924.
No manufacturer listed.

Palace in St. Petersburg to present a petition to the tsar. (Protestors were demanding an end to the disastrous Russo-Japanese War, as well as universal suffrage.) Official estimates count 130 people dead and hundreds wounded. "Bloody Sunday, as it became known, provided a focal point for discontent across the country," Mathew points out. "With little possibility of publicizing news of the killings in the press, illegally produced picture postcards became one of few ways that the population could get to see the other side of the story."[17] As protests spread across the Empire, postcards followed. Postcards that had once helped establish a national narrative could now help undercut it. As imperial Russia continued to sputter along over the next decade and a half, postcards continued to mark its downfall. After the 1917 Bolshevik Revolution, imperial Russia emerged as the Russian Soviet Federative

Socialist Republic. Over the next five years, its expansion transformed Eurasian geopolitics and national boundaries.

Revolutionary groups specifically used postcards for "correspondence, fundraising, and propaganda purposes," Alison Rowley observes.[18] Postcards allowed a form of self-presentation for groups that traditional media coverage did not. They offered a visual text to specifically target sympathizers outside of Russia who would, revolutionaries felt, offer crucial financial and ideological support. Unstaged picture postcards were a powerful visual rhetoric to garner such help.

Internally, postcards served as a photojournalism of sorts, again, much in the same way as "real picture" or "real photo" postcards functioned during the Mexican Revolution. By 1917 in Petrograd (now St. Petersburg), the producers of the newspaper *Izvestiia Petrogradskogo Soveta* sold picture postcards at kiosks and railway stations, in addition to newspapers. Postcards with portraits and stories of the revolution's myriad martyr-heroes and martyr-heroines helped fix their stories in the public's mind and in the emerging national narrative. And as different revolutionary factions maneuvered for power between 1905 and 1917, postcards were inevitably part of those power plays.

By 1918 Bolshevik postcards had begun to lay claim to specific, iconic revolutionary figures through postcards. "Picture postcards were an integral part of the early cult of Lenin," Rowley says, "when portraits of him served as a legitimizing force for the regime."[19] When Lenin suffered his first stroke in 1922, his health remained precarious until his death in 1924. Picture postcards with photographs of Lenin in brilliant health were used to help create a national narrative that he was still going about the business of running the country. When Lenin died, picture postcards became part of the official mourning process as commemorative postcards and albums were rushed into production. More than just memorabilia, postcards with photographs of the long funeral procession in Lenin's honor offered further proof of how postcards were another part of the performance of public mourning. And postcards of the Lenin Mausoleum in Moscow extended the powerful

Soviet nation-building with images of Soviet citizens queued up to visit Lenin's tomb. It's difficult to understate the power of postcards and propaganda in early Soviet nation-building.

Just as the Romanov family used picture postcards to bolster their celebrity in the last years of imperial Russia, Soviet leaders turned to the popular medium as a way of generating a national narrative and shoring up political cachet. Portraits of Stalin and Lenin were ever-popular motifs, of course, as were Soviet citizens engaging in nation-building enterprises, which created a new caste of celebrity. (Postcards from the late 1930s that featured women flying, gliding, and parachute jumping were particularly powerful pieces of propaganda; between a quarter and a third of pilots trained by Soviet air clubs in the 1930s were women.) Singers, dancers, actresses, scientists, you name it—state-sponsored celebrities could, and would, be circulated throughout the USSR via postcards, as were state-sponsored building projects, transportation, and massive infrastructure projects. Postcards with images of Soviet empire-building were cheap propaganda as the USSR established an internal autocracy and projected itself to the rest of the world.

But in a post-USSR world, where are these postcards today? As with most postcards the world over, they're in nooks and crannies, cupboards and attics, shoeboxes and archives. Some have been formally accessioned to historical institutions and others find themselves part of family collections. Some are readily available and accessible; others are lost simply because they were never saved or collected.

As the geography of imperial Russia changed and expanded into the Union of Soviet Socialist Republics, the USSR ultimately included the Bukharan People's Soviet Republic, Byelorussian Soviet Socialist Republic, Estonia, parts of what is now Finland (specifically Karelia), the Khorezm People's Soviet Republic, parts of the Kingdom of Romania, Latvia, Lithuania, Russian Soviet Federative Socialist Republic, parts of what is now Poland, the Transcaucasian Soviet Federative Socialist Republic, the Tuvan People's Republic, and the Ukrainian Soviet

Socialist Republic. But other territories, regions, and states experienced a geo-political flexibility as the USSR itself expanded—they make a litany of dead countries, each with their own postcards and role in building different nationalist narratives.

Take, for example, North Ingermanland. Also known as the Republic of North Ingria and the Republic of Kirjasalo, the country was located between the Neva River and Finland, just north of St. Petersburg. Thanks to a provision in the 1721 Treaty of Nystadt, imperial Russia acquired Livonia, Estonia, Ingermanland, part of Karelia, and certain islands after a protracted war with the Kingdom of Sweden.[20] Incidentally, nations and territories mentioned in this treaty are themselves a series of long-dead countries—the places themselves, of course, remain.

At the beginning of the twentieth century, North Ingermanland broke with the Soviet authority, establishing itself as an autonomous country on January 23, 1919, with hopes of being incorporated into what was then the Kingdom of Finland. On December 5, 1920, it was re-annexed into the USSR after Finland and Soviet Russia signed the Peace Treaty of Tartu. Postcards from the region are a little bit more tricky to sort out—being a country for only a year meant that there wasn't a lot of tourism and infrastructure that could support postcards of a uniquely North Ingermanland identity, particularly as it had political aspirations of joining a different empire. "Projecting only images of social harmony," Rowley argues, "[picture postcards] suggested that Russian imperialism fostered no local resistance."[21] History reminds us that absences from the record are often just as deliberate as carefully curated propaganda.

Trying to track down postcards from places like North Ingermanland is only possible by looking in collections that have been designated as "Finnish" or "Russian." The country simply shows up in the geographical and political reorganization that followed it historically. Indeed, a postcard from "Minsk, Russia" that was published as a curiosity in the local *Middleton Transcript* newspaper in Middleton, Delaware, in 1917, described the postcard as being written in English, Russian, and Yiddish

New York Public Library postcard drawers by location,
illustrating historical geography.

from the "great Revolution in Russia." Tracing the postcard today would be difficult, as Minsk is now the capital of Belarus.[22] These material traces of former geographies are reminders that the countries, nations, and empires of the twentieth century were dynamic political entities.

"Today, a large number of Russian postcards remain in private hands rather than in public collections maintained by libraries and archives," Rowley observes. "Once treasured parts of individual collections, the postcards are slowly being discarded or sold off as grandchildren and great-grandchildren fail to see the value of such 'clutter' except perhaps in monetary terms."[23] Although personal collections might be at the mercy of familial decluttering, the broader collecting community of postcards—deltiologists—has been foundational in building scholarly understanding of different subsets of Russian revolutionary as well as anti-government postcards.[24]

Postcards that bridged the space between imperial Russia and the USSR offered views of an emerging economy, national narratives, tourism development, and of course, attempts to formalize how citizens performed their patriotism, one postcard at a time.

. . . .

Traces of historical geography inevitably turn up in collections. Personal collections will have postcards saved from such countries, of course, as will the occasional eBay seller. (This is the "clutter" that Rowley described.) Pulling together formal, searchable collections of postcards from countries that don't exist anymore is a bit tricky. But the Picture Collection held at the New York Public Library offers a way into this question of historical geography. This collection got its formal start in 1915, during the Golden Age of postcards. It contains roughly 1 million prints, photographs, and posters as well as illustrations from books, magazines, and newspapers.

New York Public Library patrons are allowed to check out historic postcards from a subset of the Picture Collection's cache ("circulating postcards" as opposed to "reference postcards"), just as they would any other library text. (Signs on top of the collection's cabinets explain how this works. "May be borrowed or copied." "Limit of 15 postcards each checkout." "Return postcards to information desk after use.") It's as though the library has put its collection of postcards back into circulation long after the postcards were received and read by their original recipients.

"We have a lot of design and fashion students who check out vintage postcards," Jessica Cline, the supervising librarian for the Picture Collection, remarked as we chatted across the table in the collection room. She had pulled some of her favorites to show me the range of postcards in the collection. Raymond Khan, a senior librarian with the Picture Collection and Cline's colleague, joined us. "The vintage cards can really help evoke a certain era or ethos."[25]

The postcards themselves are housed in black, metal filing cabinets with long, narrow drawers, which were purchased in the mid-twentieth century. ("These drawers are **heavy**," a printout warns visitors. "Please use caution when opening them.") All of the postcards used to be housed at the Mid-Manhattan Library, which is where I first came across the postcard collection, by happenstance, several years ago. Eventually, the collection was relocated to the library's Stephen A. Schwarzman Building. The postcards are a resource for students, but they're also a way for casual visitors to see what sorts of texts are in the Picture Collection. When visitors—"tourists, usually," Cline smiles—wander into room 100 on the Schwarzman's first floor, librarians invite and encourage them to peruse the cabinets of postcards. "People are drawn to postcards of places that they live. People always look up postcards of where they're from," Cline said. "Always."[26]

There are thousands of postcards in the cabinets, organized more or less geographically, by the origin of the postcard, or at least where it was sent from. This makes sense. Geography and place are an inherent part of a postcard and have been since postcards were first popped into the post. "Tourists come from all over the world to visit the New York Public Library," librarian Jay Vissers observes. "As soon as they find

תל-אביב—רחוב יהודה הלוי
Tel-Aviv — Jehuda-Halevi Str.

Two windmills in the Netherlands; the exact geographic
location is ambiguous. Printed 1890–1900.

Postcard from Tel Aviv, then in "Mandatory Palestine" (today Israel),
c. 1920s. Edition Moshe Ordmann No. 4–Tel-Aviv–Jehuda-Halevi Str.

PAGODA PARK IN SEOUL, COREA.　韓國京城パゴダ公園

Pagoda Park in Seoul, Korea (today South Korea). Postcard printed *c.* 1904.

The Great Forest, near city of Debreczin (Debrecen),
Austro-Hungary (today Hungary). Printed 1890–1900.

out we have postcards, they immediately want to see postcards of their country. It's like they want to see the image that Americans have of where the tourists come from."[27]

The top, first drawer on the left side of wall of postcard-filled cabinets has a neat, handwritten label that reads "AFGHANISTAN—AUSTRIA—hotels and restaurants." The next drawer has postcards from "AUSTRIA— (A-L)—BOSNIA & HERZEGOVINA." The drawers continue to take visitors through the world's geography (for example, "FRANCE—A—FRANCE—Chamonix") with drawers specifically devoted to particularly popular places, buildings, or subjects ("PARIS—Museums—Louvre.") Some drawers offer odd juxtapositions of geography and alphabetical order. ("LONDON—stores—MAINE—rivers.") There are beaches, forests, vistas, museums, cathedrals, and peoples all connected through the twist of fate that brought the postcards to their current place in the collection.

"Acquisition has been mainly through donations from hobbyists and travelers, but the department has historically sought ways to harvest ephemeral material of this kind," the NYPL digital collections website offers as an explanation of where their thousands of postcards come from. "Librarians on foreign or domestic travels, for instance, are encouraged to buy and add postcards to the collection."[28]

Serendipity is no stranger to the twists of postcard geography. Jay Vissers chimed in: "We had a couple from Spain once who had come to New York and looked up postcards from where they lived. They found a postcard with a picture of their house on it. Their house!" Vissers shook his head at the improbability of it all. "They said, 'We didn't know that there was a postcard of our house!' If this were a movie, you wouldn't believe it."[29]

So pick a drawer, any drawer—there are postcards from anywhere and everywhere in the world. At one point in my visit, I pulled open a drawer to explore postcards from the American Midwest and postcards from "NEBRASKA—A-Z"; "LINCOLN (STATE CAPITAL)"; "OMAHA"; also "NETHERLANDS—A-Z." Visitors will find the postcards are subdivided by geographic subject and separated by tabbed manila dividers penned in the same neat handwriting as the front of the cabinet drawers. The deliberate, precisely spaced capital letters on the sub-dividers show how the postcards have been organized through geography over decades.

But look closely. There is more to the geography than meets the eye, because we can find subtle changes to the dividers in every filing cabinet. Some names have changed. ("MYANMAR (BURMA).") Visitors come across plenty of countries that don't exist anymore. ("CZECHO-SLOVAKIA.") It's as though we're seeing a microcosm of history and geopolitics all neatly organized, picture postcard by picture postcard, as nations come and go in the twentieth century. We can see that nations, states, and borders are not static entities. ("MACEDONIA.") Rather, they are dynamic, complex political entities—and their respective postcards reflect that. ("CHINA—PEKING Forbidden City.") Postcards are perfect proxies for this historical phenomenon because postcards aren't only about place. They're about time as well.

Some of the Picture Collection's country sub-dividers have simply been turned over and reused. The back of the card for "SRI LANKA," for example, is labeled "CEYLON," as the island off the coast of southern India was formerly known to the West, having been a British colony until its political independence in 1948. The postcards in that category haven't changed and haven't been re-classified; it's just the country's name that's different. Today, it's easy to see these categories and country names as vestiges of twentieth-century colonialism and imperialism. Postcards themselves were just as much about connecting colonies with metropoles and the spread of an identifying national narrative as they were about tourism, travel, and holiday greetings.

New dividers in the cabinet drawers have been added by staff and volunteers over the years to continue to update the labels for countries and places. "MYANMAR—Life" might be a newly named divider, but the historic postcards in the MYANMAR section have "Burma" typeset across the front of the postcard as it was printed decades ago. "Geographic destinations (like all of our subject headings) are updated by the librarians

Postcard from Tuva, USSR, 1967.

Postcard of Mount Kazbek, Gergeti Trinity Church, and Georgian countryside
along the Georgian Military Road (then part of the Russian Empire),
Detroit Publishing Company, printed 1890–1900.

as soon as they come to our attention," Cline explained.[30] The more
we dig in to how the collection is organized, the more we realize that
the postcards show us a plethora of cultural stratas—layers of stories
on top of other stories. Through the collection, we find new countries,
different names, political revolution, social reorganization, censorship,
and international tourism. All through an ever-evolving system to index
the world's geopolitics via postcards.

Reading through the messages on postcards from countries that
don't exist anymore feels a bit like reading through translations of ancient cuneiform tablets. There was an almost banal familiarity to the
written messages, much like contemporary text messages. ("Please save
the card," a message on a postcard from Zagreb read, dated to 1977.)
But the countries and the cultural context are completely different from

what we would find at that latitude and longitude today. It's not just that nations have changed over the twentieth century, switching one name out for another. It's that their geo-political boundaries are created, live for a little while, and then die.

Many of these nation-states do not exist anymore, but their postcards turn up in curious and unexpected places. These, like any and every other sort of postcard, can be read as political propaganda, scenic landscapes, tourist enticements, and celebrity portraits. But more than anything, postcards from dead countries are social connections between people within an empire as well as how people linked themselves to the rest of the world. Postcards offer a way to see how now-dead countries were connected through a global social network.

. . . .

By their very nature, postcards tell us about geography—they have to be sent from one place to another—but here in the twenty-first century, they offer a means of finding and remembering hidden geographies of countries that don't exist anymore. They are snippets that offer a cultural history that can't be found through other media and material culture. Postcards from dead countries are ways of tracing colonialism, empire, and the fluid contingency of geography and history.

The now-dead country of Tannu Tuva is one such dead country geography. It was formally recognized between 1921 and 1944 before it was annexed to the USSR. Prior to that, the region (then known as Tuva) had been a protectorate of imperial Russia and in the eighteenth century had been considered part of Mongolia. Located at the geographic center of the Asian continent, its political history is complicated as larger empires (Russian, Mongolian, and Chinese) have all vied to include Tuva as a means of shoring up their own respective boundaries. (Incidentally, "Tuva" has had seven centuries of postal communications—social networks that are much older than the modern nation-states.[31])

Popular interest in Tannu Tuva was revived in the late twentieth century thanks to famous physicist Richard Feynman's attempt to visit in the 1980s. The effort was chronicled by Feynman's friend and high school teacher Ralph Leighton (*Tuva or Bust!*) I couldn't resist the impulse to load up eBay and see what postcards I could find—if any—from Tuva. (I wasn't finding postcards from Tuva in archives and public collections, so perhaps, I reasoned, the Internet's yard sale approach to buying and selling kitsch could offer something.) And eBay did not disappoint. I bought a "RARE Soviet TUVA USSR State Emblem Coast & Flag SIBERIA 1967 Postcard." I think that this is as close as I will come to finding a postcard from Tuva, USSR-era or not.

The postcard had an official Soviet emblem on the front and Tuva's flag (itself Central Asian-inspired motifs); the back of the postcard informed me "напечатано в сссп" (Made in the USSR), the postcard had been printed at the Moscow Printing Factory of Goznak, and it cost 6 kopeks in 1967. In early 2020, it cost $4.75 to ship from Russia and the seller (Olga) promised it would arrive in mere weeks.

Back in the New York Public Library Picture Collection, the Soviet-era postcards offer more insight about the of geographical contingency of changing nations and countries. There were dividers in the collection labeled "CRIMEA (SSR) SEVASTOPOL" as well as "RUSSIA—ESTONIA (SSR)." Crimea was annexed by the Russian Empire in 1783, became an autonomous republic in 1917, and in 1954 was transferred to Ukraine SSR, after the entire indigenous population of Crimean Tatars were deported to Central Asia in an act of genocide. Here in the twenty-first century, the question is far from settled, as the Autonomous Republic of Crimea was annexed by the Russian Federation in 2014. The Picture Collection has opted to keep the group of postcards labeled as CRIMEA (SSR) SEVASTOPOL, thus underscoring the historical context of those specific postcards. It might be a dead country by stamp-collecting standards, but it's a live, dynamic region, and the postcards from CRIMEA (SSR) remind us that the politics of geography have been inexorably tangled in the history of power and empire for over a century.

....

Виды Туркестана. Самаркандъ. Древняя мечеть.

Postcard from Samarkand, c. 1912, then part of the Russian Empire's expansion into Central Asia, today Uzbekistan. The text is in Russian rather than Uzbek.

Postcard from Samarkand, Uzbekistan. The author mailed it to her spouse from Samarkand in 2003. Though almost 100 years later than the postcard of Uzbekistan shown earlier, the cards offer a similar aesthetic.

Eastern Karelia lasted only a few weeks during the Soviet-Finnish War of 1922. The Orange Free State (a Boer republic in South Africa) stood half a century as an independent country in the late 1800s. The Scandinavian state of Schleswig lasted from 1864 until 1867; the Danish West Indies existed for over 160 years. "History is littered with the corpses of would-be states that never made it, empires that dissolved and recognized countries that disappeared into the embraces of more powerful neighbors," geographer Nick Middleton reflects.[32] And postcards track the geopolitical turnover that came about in the nineteenth and twentieth centuries through revolution, turmoil, or just plain nation-building.

Postcards offer personal connections to geography and place. "When people find postcards of where they're from, there's a sense of 'This postcard represents me or my place,'" librarian Jessica Cline observes, reflecting on the visitors to the New York Public Library's Picture Collection.[33] A postcard is a material thing—a tangible object that can be physically tied to a place on a map as well as a national identity.

As I looked through the collection, focusing on postcards from countries that don't exist anymore, I realized that the artistic composition and subject matter of those postcards were surprisingly unsurprising. I'm not sure what I expected to find, really. "I knew I was not alone in feeling lost, but I had to understand how others processed the same collective experience we had as a fragmented nation," travel writer Anja Mutic offered in 2018, trying to make sense of her visit to the six countries that formerly made up Yugoslavia, the country of her birth, more than twenty years after the country collapsed.[34]

Such a sense of nostalgia or closure might come, I would venture to guess, as postcards from such countries are encountered by former residents decades later. "When tourists come visit the New York Public Library postcard collection and check out postcards from their home countries, they point out different things on the postcards to their children," Jay Vissers points out. "Like 'This is what used to be here, and I remember going here and here.'" He paused. "There's a lot of reminiscing that happens when tourists look at postcards from their home countries."[35]

Postcards from dead countries offer material accounts of social and political change. They let us see individuals who were part of the birth, life, and death of countries as well as the grand, national narratives that postcard propaganda builds. Postcards are artifacts tied to places and times that no longer exist.

CONCLUSION:
THE AFTERLIVES
OF POSTCARDS

·····················

On July 9, 1956, American writer Jack Kerouac had had enough. Earlier that year, Viking Press had expressed an interest in acquiring the Beat writer's manuscript for *On the Road*, but dithered for months without offering Kerouac a formal contract. Since Kerouac had been writing and revising *On the Road* for years, he grew frustrated as he watched the manuscript languish in the publishing house; Malcolm Cowley, one of Viking's editorial consultants and Kerouac's point of contact, didn't seem to be in a hurry to move the acquisition along.

Which is why, on that Monday in July 1956, Kerouac mailed Cowley a classic-looking Curt Teich & Co. postcard that had an idyllic view of the Lower Falls in Yellowstone National Park on the front and a particularly blunt, scathing message on the back.

Dear Malcolm- You've all delayed once more, not sending my work for the summer on the mountain—I've started an epic novel of 1000 pages THE BEAT GENERATION—**If you don't send me a contract with an advance (or some kind of option) by October first on ON THE ROAD, I am going to withdraw the manuscript from Viking** and sell it elsewhere. Than have it demeaned I'd rather it were never published.—Period.

Jack Kerouac[1]

Incidentally, Viking published *On The Road* the following year.

Over six decades later, Kerouac's postcard lives on as a classic in online listicles that feature collections of "postcards from famous writers" and images of the postcard are mainstays of Tumblr posts about all things Beat Generation. The physical postcard itself has been saved and curated as part of a collection of Cowley's papers held in the Newberry Library in Chicago.

. . . .

After a postcard has been sent, received, and read, then what? What happens to postcards after their original circulation?

This is where the afterlife of postcards begins. Some postcards, especially advertisements or the like, were tossed soon after delivery as the message or ad would have been received immediately. But many postcards were personal, and this meant that they were saved—in some way—by the recipient. Postcards might be kept so the addressee can read and reread the postcard's message. The act of saving a postcard becomes a physical manifestation of the remaining connection between sender and recipient. Throwing away the postcard—ephemeral and disposable though it is—feels like throwing away that personal connection. There's a sentimentality and sociability that keeping postcards satisfies.

Often "saving" postcards is completely haphazard. Postcards can easily be stuck in books, slide in with jumbles of letters and photographs, or just sort of float along in desk drawers and pop up in unexpected places. For example, Sheila Liming, an English literature professor who studies American writer Edith Wharton, told me about finding several postcards stuck in Wharton's personal books either by Wharton herself or stewards of her book collection, like twentieth-century art critic Kenneth Clark, who inherited part of Wharton's library. "It's so

Embroidered postcards from the First World War purchased in France by the author's great-grandfather George Sandberg, 1917–18. Postcards served a variety of functions beyond simply being an inexpensive communication: this one was an unmailed souvenir.

charming to think of Kenneth Clark—an esteemed critic, television personality, and the owner of a castle (not to mention a very fine art collection)—playing the role of the tourist," Liming says, pointing to a postcard from 1975 that she found decades later tucked in a book while digitizing the Wharton collection.[2]

Over time, saved postcards begin to accumulate as they fill shoeboxes and albums. Ascribing meaning or intentionality to the cache is perplexing as the personal connections are lost. But as their immediate connections fade, their cachet as historical artifacts begins to rise and their age imbues them with a sense that they ought to be saved. More than anything else, here in the twenty-first century, people seem to be unsure of what to do with their personal, relict family collections of postcards. Several historians, researchers, artists, and scholars whom I interviewed for this book spoke about having these collections of family postcards and not being really sure what to do with them, regardless of whether or not they have the physical space to store them. Keeping them is often easier than finding a socially acceptable way of offloading them. ("I feel like they ought to go somewhere," one colleague offered. "They're so useful to understanding the early twentieth century. Personally, I just don't want to keep them, but I can't quite make myself get rid of them either.") Another colleague pointed out that they're constantly "gifted" with old postcards as others clean out closets and attics as they happened to have worked on postcards for a project. Long after they were originally sent and received, postcards are recirculating through the material continuum of the twenty-first century.

Saving postcards is one thing; actively collecting them is another. Collecting has been part of postcards from their beginning. Recall that postcards were often sold in sets—like those from fundraising efforts for the women's suffrage movement or picked up as mementos to mark a visit to a tourist destination, like Mark Twain's set of postcards from his trip to Warwick Castle in England. (Some of the earliest vending machines were set up to sell sets of postcards to either send or collect; these sets were particularly popular among tourists.) Postcards were made to be bought, sent, and received, but they were also made to be collected, and postcard albums were popular tools for carefully keeping them, if one was looking for something more methodical than the haphazardness of a shoebox. In 1909, for example, postcard albums were advertised in local papers—25 cents for an album that would hold a hundred postcards and $1.75 would buy a collector a red leather, gold-stamped album that could hold four hundred.[3] When the craze for collecting picture postcards was well on its way in Europe (c. 1890s), postcard clubs and societies were common and members could exchange cards with each other or with other members overseas.[4] Postcards could thus be collected either before or after sending them—a collector would simply be keeping the postcard at a different stage in the postcard's afterlife.

Even though blank postcards can start out similar to each other—say, postcard copies made during the same print run—it's what happens after the printing that makes them unique and gives them the reason to be saved or collected. They're sold to different people, mailed to different places. "Each postcard is an original idea, not an illustration," poet and publisher Thomas A. Clark offers in his 2000 essay "By the Morning Post" about an exhibition of postcards designed by Scottish artist Ian Hamilton Finlay. "If you own one of these postcards, you own an original work by this artist. Instead of acting as a reminder of something that exists somewhere else, that you may or may not have seen, it shares the same space as you, addressing you directly."[5]

So what makes a postcard collection a collection, and not just an arbitrary cache? Collections of postcards, like any collection of objects, have always been about what they represent to the collector. "Collecting is a curious behavior. Almost everyone has formed a collection, however small," professor of art crime Erin Thompson argues in *Possession: The Curious History of Private Collectors from Antiquity to the Present*. "There are collectors for every category of object, natural and artificial, from Fabergé eggs to nail clippings. We find such collections throughout human history."[6]

Albums were popular places to organize and store postcards
at the beginning of the 20th century, *c.* 1910–20.

These holiday postcards were stored grouped together in an album, *c.* 1910–20.

Collections of postcards are everywhere and come in all sorts. Books about postcards curate particular genres or offer readers a sort of catalog of particular scenes or types of postcards. Some formal collections are governed by the same financial motivations as collectors of rare art and books. Other formal collectors focus on completing a particular print run of postcards or reaggregating a postcard set. Exhibitions that offer audiences a slice of history, like the 2018 exhibition *From Madras to Bangalore* at the University of London, told through postcard imagery, walk a fine line between curations and collections. ("Part of the fascination of collecting suffrage cards is our ability to see and analyze these pre-Twitter reactions to history," historian Kenneth Florey offers.[7]) Just as there are a multitude of postcards that history has seen, there are infinite ways to collect them. However niche a subset of postcards might appear, I can guarantee you, reader, that someone, somewhere, has collected them.

Postcard collections can thus be comprised of anything the collector finds meaningful. (A collector from the Victorian era, for example, would have kept postcards for very different reasons than a twenty-first century archivist.) Because postcards are fundamentally non-scarce objects, the hows and whys of postcard collections are as diverse and myriad as the subjects, printings, and genres of postcards themselves.

....

For the private collector who treats collections as a form of financial, historical, or cultural investment rather than a set of mementos, there's an ever-ready market for buying and collecting celebrity ephemera, and it would seem that postcards are far from immune to that. The 1840 postcard that is credited with being the "first" postcard drawn and sent by Theodore Hook, Esq., Fulham, offered private collectors a singular piece of postal history when it went to auction in 2002. ("The hammer went down at £27,000 but the total price including commission and value added tax [VAT] was £31,750," the BBC reported of the record sale.[8])

Postcards that offer collectors a brush with celebrity certainly make it easy to understand why people collect them over the hundreds of billions of others that have ever existed. In September 2014, Skinner Inc. put to auction a newly discovered cache of Jack Kerouac ephemera that dated as far back as 1939. The auction included seventeen complete letters, two postcards, and seven "substantial fragments" that "sustained significant damage from a leaking paint can," as the *Los Angeles Times* reported. "While some details of the auction are still being finalized, the 17 letters will be sold as separate lots with estimated values of $2,000 to $5,000 apiece."[9] As estimates of Kerouac's estate come in around $30 million, it's easy to see that the value of the postcards isn't just in their age (I could buy similarly styled vintage postcards from eBay for a couple of dollars), but in the fact they'd been in the possession of Kerouac himself.

And it's not just celebrity that makes for expensive collectible post-cards—it turns out that notoriety will do nicely as well. In April 2018, for example, a postcard believed to have been sent by Jack the Ripper went to auction. The card had belonged to a Metropolitan Police constable who, as the BBC reports, was given the postcard as a memento when he retired from the force in 1866, and had later been passsed on to his widow. The auctioneers stated, "The card is definitely of the period and has police provenance."

The postcard is dated October 29, 1888 and is addressed in large script "To the High Street Ealing Police Station Sergent [*sic*]." The postcard is rather small, even by postcard standards; it measures 2¾ inches by 4¾ inches (7 × 12 cm). A halfpenny stamp showing Queen Victoria's profile is canceled on the upper right corner of the address side of the postcard—this is a postcard that predates cards with images and divided backs—and the reverse side reads, "Beware there is two women I want here and I mean to have them my knife is still in good order it is a students knife and I hope you liked the kidney. I am Jack the Ripper." The auction house Grand Auctions in Folkestone, Kent, estimated that the postcard might fetch somewhere between £600 and £900. It sold for £22,000 after a British private collector "won a bidding war with an American for the rare letter."[10]

Again, a postcard with a singular life history that appeals to a general cultural gestalt—something that sets that one postcard apart from the myriad of others that look exactly like it—often translates to a reason for that one postcard to be collected. Artist and writer Jeremy Cooper, for example, spent six years carefully curating a collection of postcards by famous mid- to late twentieth-century artists, from John Lennon and Yoko Ono to Jasper Johns. Cooper's collection even boasted some postcards from the 1980s that were full of "caustic feminist graffiti sprayed on to billboard ads," ArtDaily.com reported.[11]

But all of the different genres of postcards had passed through artists' hands as an informing part of their art in some way, and in turn informed Cooper's collection. In 2019 the British Museum showed three hundred of the postcards from the Cooper collection in the exhibition *The World Exists to Be Put on a Postcard*. The Cooper collection of postcards was collected with the intent of eventually being donated to an institution that would hold them in public trust.

"So what does motivate the collector?" art historian Erin Thompson presses. "Finding out is crucial, because collections can shape our perception of the world, knowledge of its past, and course of its future."[12] Most collectors today tend to focus their efforts into three major categories: places (geographies, landscapes, and the like or "topographical views"); artistic cards (what some collectors call "miniature art galleries"); and subjects ("transportation" or "monuments.") Specific trends and tastes change over time and what's in fashion for collectors varies. But, for many collectors, the power of the physical media resonates more than just seeing images of postcards online. What's collected might change, but the collecting behavior endures.

"I think it's a bit like vinyl music," Brian Lund, who has been editor and publisher of *Picture Postcard Monthly* for 35 years, explained to me in an interview. "There's something that is particularly personal about owning music rather than streaming it and I think postcards have that same sort of connection to collectors. It translates to younger generations." Lund also emphasized the personal material connection that he finds in connecting postcards with collectors. "Postcards survive very well," he points out, despite postcards being a "disposable" medium. Just as a postcard's original connection was personal, so it is when it is recirculated.[13]

There are concerns among collecting circles that interest in postcard collecting—like postcards themselves—is waning, particularly among the casual collector, and postcards are now the third most likely item to be collected in the United States, behind stamps and coins, though they used to rank even higher in popularity. The biggest contemporary collectors are institutions—places like archives and libraries—where postcards add to the material artifacts already there. Some collections, like Jeremy Cooper's, are formally accessioned and will live on, as do other works of art or artifacts that are available to the institutions' audiences. The Musée de la Carte Postale (Museum of Postcards) in Antibes, France, displays thousands and thousands of postcards for its visitors.

Yet other collections of postcards—like the massive Curt Teich one held at the Newberry Library—serve as a historical register for the industry. When I wanted to tell my niece the age of the Curt Teich postcard from Provo, Utah, that I sent her, I looked up the postcard's serial number online. That collection serves as a historical guidepost for professional collectors as well as academic and independent researchers. I did, of course, imply that because the postcard was so old, I certainly hoped she would save it; thus the cycle of collecting continues. In other words, postcard collections beget postcard collections.

. . . .

Saving and collecting isn't the only afterlife available to postcards. Here in the twenty-first century, postcards have found new niches—in art, iconography, and as a specific form of "slow communication" to challenge the assumption that omnipresent digital "nowness" is how messages ought to be sent and received. While people might not send postcards as much as they once did, there are myriad ways that postcards resonate. Postcards are still a material form and cultural symbol of communication.

I come back to the question, "Do people even send postcards anymore?" And while "no," people don't send them as much as they did, the answer is also "yes." People still send postcards, and for many of the same reasons that they have for decades—postcards are personal, they tell stories, and they connect people across geographies. Postcards might not be sent by the hundreds of billions in the twenty-first century, but they still connect people through a material social network. (That personal connection is what makes them unique and compelling. One example of uniquely twenty-first century postcards is the Postcards to Voters project: "friendly, handwritten reminders from volunteers to targeted voters giving Democrats a winning edge in close, key races

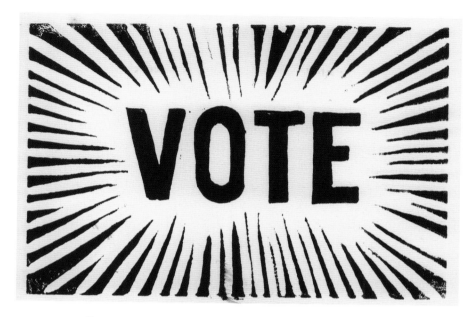

Postcard for "Get Out the Vote" efforts in the United States, 2016.

coast to coast," the postcard project's website explains.[14]) In other words, the personal connection between sender and recipient carries a cachet that email listservs, tweets, and Instagram posts simply do not.

But more than just sending new postcards, the twenty-first century offers old postcards a new afterlife by recirculating them through art and craft. Etsy shop artisans, for example, offer cutesy ways for vintage postcards to be cut up and remade into new shabby-chic crafts or offer "reprintings" of iconic postcard art. Contemporary British photographer Martin Parr has published a collection of "boring" postcards that individually are indeed pedestrian and banal but when taken together offer a visual, social history of Britain. American contemporary artists Suzanne Bloom and Ed Hill use postcards in their *Now and Then* project—a series that emphasizes the enduring cultural effects of mass media. Their photographs of postcards are a way for the postcards that they've received or collected over the years to recirculate to new viewers.[15]

An original postcard that might have been bought, signed, and sent decades ago may now circulate through another—broader—set of audiences. Present-day audiences understand the iconography of postcards—tourism, propaganda, geographic distancing—and that cultural shorthand makes postcards easily recognized symbols in present-day art. The art world's use of postcards draws heavily from the social symbolism, geographic connections, and iconography of communication that postcards convey. Even if someone has never sent or received a postcard—even if someone has never physically interacted with that social network or that print media—there's a sense of what a postcard ought to do.

It's this ethos of print that American artist Zoe Leonard's massive postcard installation *You see I am here after all* (2008) taps into. The piece showcases 3,851 vintage postcards from Niagara Falls. The Whitney Museum of American Art in New York City showcased *You see I am here after all* as part of "Survey," a large-scale overview of Leonard's work on exhibition between March 2 and June 10, 2018. A collection of postcards, Leonard's work suggests, does more than just save or curate postcards as artifacts. It carries a purpose and an aesthetic intentionality that merges history, culture, and technology.

Overall, *You see I am here after all* measures something like 11 feet, 10½ inches by 147 feet (3.62 by 44.8 meters) once the postcards are fully installed. What strikes viewers immediately is the size and scale of the piece—dimensions that, perhaps, mimic the social expanse and network of postcards themselves. The postcards are immediately identifiable as postcards (their iconic size and shape is a giveaway, to say nothing of the images' brightly saturated hues), but it takes a closer examination of the postcards in *You see I am here after all* to really put it together that these were all postcards of a landscape as famous as Niagara Falls. Helpfully, some of the different postcard printings tell you what scene the postcard offers, right there on the front of the card, such as "View from Prospect Point," "American Falls from Luna Island, Showing New Rainbow Bridge," and "Horseshoe Falls."[16]

The postcards in *You see I am here after all* are clustered and hung based on a fine-grained typology, almost as if Leonard is creating a formal archeological seriation. The different color blocks immediately stand out—there are some parts of the installation that are more blue, some that share tinges of an old-timey sepia. Some postcards are displayed in their traditional horizontal landscape mode; a few sets of postcards are actually oriented vertically to capture the size and scale of the waterfalls. But each "type" of postcard is nestled, gridded, and displayed with other postcards just like it. Once viewers start parsing the intricacies of *You see I am here after all*, it's clear that Leonard is walking her visitors through a history of Niagara Falls, told through different postcard technologies and decades' worth of mailed missives. And viewers quickly appreciate that although these are artifacts of mass production, no two are exactly the same. If you look closely, you can see that some postcards have rounded corners, others have messages written across them. Some have postmarks stamped on the front. Others show bends and creases—the wear and tear that time exerts on a disposable medium like postcards.

The original senders of these postcards could not possibly have imagined that, decades later, their postcards would have been so repurposed and reframed. It's impossible to stand in front of the wall installations and not imagine the hundreds—thousands—of messages that have been sent and received through just this one set of views, be they from Virginia or Niagara Falls. Take a close look at any one of the postcards individually, and you can catch a snippet of someone's life—because the sender opted to write the message on the front of the postcard, rather than on the back. ("July 22, 1907. Dear Stella:—How would you like to see this? Send me a card and I will do the same as soon as I go to Clayton. Love to you all. Yours, Lizzie.") Since the postcards are mounted with the images out, it's impossible to see where the messages were sent—but we can assume that all of them originated at the tourist point in question. Leonard's work offers a new life for these artifacts, turning them into unique collections of material social history.

Niagara Falls from Prospect Point. Detroit Publishing Company, 1898–1931.
Postcards from this image series were used in Zoe Leonard's installation *You see I am here after all*, 2008.

We come back to the point that postcards require participation: A sender must fill out the back of the card and send it in the mail—to say nothing of buying it in the first place. In every instance in which postcards are recirculated, their afterlife still requires participation. Collections in libraries, archives, art, craft, and shoeboxes full of family postcards still require that people participate and circulate them for the picture cards to be, well, postcards.

. . . .

It felt impossible to write a book about postcards—and to claim that they were a mass medium that required personal participation—without sending them en masse myself. What would it look like, I wondered, to use postcards as an everyday piece of written communication when they're not quite as common as they once were? And to do so well into the twenty-first century, where posted mail is itself quaint and sending a postcard would require more deliberate effort than simply sending a text message? What could I understand about postcards by sending

Contemporary postcard designed and mailed
by the author's nephew, Colten Brewer, age 11, 2019.

them that I couldn't by simply sorting through them in archives? I had come to see postcards as a defiant gesture against the onslaught of fast, digital communication—I wanted to see what it would be like to send something slow and to have to wait for a response.

I started off sending postcards of Austin, Texas-centric themes to my sister's kids in Arizona because I wanted to show them what the city looked like. (The capital building, Lady Bird Lake, Austin City Limits music festival, the bat colony at Congress Street bridge, to name a few.) The Gen Z kids knew what postcards were—I asked them, specifically— but they said they had never seen postcards in person, or received them. But the idea that they were picture messages sent from somewhere that was "not home" was an iconic part of the postcard, even for those who had never sent or received one. They knew what a postcard "ought" to do—carry a short message from one person to another—but offered that postcards felt different than the short messages we texted in Google Hangouts. My grandmothers, on the other hand, thought that the postcards I sent them were quite a lark; the cards were a throwback and a bit of nostalgia for written and mailed communication.

This postcard correspondence quickly picked up steam. I sent postcards to my nieces and nephew from Denmark, Italy, and France. ("I like the ones from different countries," one niece explained to me. "It makes me want to visit there some day.") I found prints of art from museums in New York and mailed them to my grandmothers. I bought postcards with snarky, brilliant puns and gleefully waited for the recipient to text me with the eye-rolling or vomit emoji once their postcard finally showed up. Postcards that I ordered from Timbuktu—after coming across the project in research for this book—could be monitored via Instagram. Sunsets, clichés, and sweeping vistas—I bought, addressed, and mailed them all. When I couldn't find physical postcards to mail from Mongolia, I simply loaded an app on my phone that would turn photos into postcards, and typed out messages' text and the recipients' address.

Sending postcards—especially this frequently, this predictably, and this systematically—hasn't been easy. For one thing, although postcards

Although it's easy to decry postcards as an extinct medium,
they still show up in the 21st century in often unexpected ways.
German postcard advertising Wikipedia, 2016.

are around, they're not around everywhere. There have been plenty
of places that I've looked for postcards and come up empty-handed.
(There was one especially sketchy gas station in Tucson, Arizona, where
I unearthed some desert-motif postcards between bottles of motor oil
and PayDay candy bars. The colors and typesetting across the front
screamed "1987." No matter. I blew off the dust and popped them in
the post.) Even places that have postcards often don't have a very large
or varied inventory. Institutions with gift shops or souvenir venues have
postcards, but it's casually encountering them that is difficult. This is
what has changed in the material lives of postcards—they are present,
but no longer ubiquitous.

As I've continued to send friends and family postcards, many have
opted to post pictures of them to Instagram or Twitter. This is yet

another afterlife of contemporary postcards—a public confirmation that a postcard message has been received. It's a bit of a historical twist that a post with a picture of a picture postcard integrates one social network with a much newer one.

While we might not send postcards at the rate and for the reasons we did in the last century, postcards have evolved to carry a unique cultural cachet. Where postcards were once seen as ephemeral and disposal (because they were everywhere), today they resonate with recipients because of the social effort that they require (finding a stamp, an address, a postbox, etc.) Postcards are a physical, material manifestation of, "Hey! I thought of you!" And posting the picture to social media becomes the social reciprocity of that thought.

. . . .

For over one hundred years, we have been hearing that postcards are a dying medium—and yet we continue to see them, encounter them, and know them, as we have done for decades. We see them literally where postcards continue to be sold, purchased, signed, and sent. We see them figuratively in twenty-first-century social media, as every meme, every selfie, every inane or important thing that anyone has ever posted on social media has at some point had a parallel appear as part of a postcard. The twenty-first century is full of postcards, as they are recirculated—both literally and figuratively—through art, symbols, iconography, and symbolism.

I would like to believe that news of postcards' death has been greatly exaggerated.

REFERENCES

· · · · · · · · · · · · · · · · · · ·

INTRODUCTION: INVENTION AND REINVENTION

1 Daniel Gifford, "Rural Americans, Postcards, and the Fiscal Transformation of the Post Office Department, 1909–1911," in *The Winton M. Blount Postal History Symposia: Selected Papers, 2010–2011* (Washington, DC, 2012), pp. 77–84.

2 Alison Rowley, phone interview, February 3, 2020.

3 Raymond Khan, interview, October 31, 2019.

4 Jia Tolentino, "The Age of Instagram Face," www.newyorker.com, December 19, 2019.

5 Daniel Gifford, *American Holiday Postcards, 1905–1915: Imagery and Context* (Jefferson, NC, 2013), p. 1.

6 Daniel Gifford, "Golden Age of Postcards," www.saturdayeveningpost.com, December 12, 2016.

7 Frank Staff, *The Picture Postcard and Its Origins*, 1st edn (London, 1966); Martin Willoughby, *A History of Postcards: A Pictorial Record from the Turn of the Century to the Present Day* (London, 1994).

8 "Postcard History," Smithsonian Institution Archives, www.siarchives.si.edu/history, September 19, 2013.

ONE SIGNED, STAMPED, AND DELIVERED

1 Daniel Gifford, "Rural Americans, Postcards, and the Fiscal Transformation of the Post Office Department, 1909–1911," in *The Winton M. Blount Postal History Symposia: Selected Papers, 2010–2011* (Washington, DC, 2012), p. 81.

2 Ibid.

3 Ibid., p. 78.

4 Michael Todd, "A Short History of Home Mail Delivery," www.psmag.com, February 6, 2013.

5 Samuel Kernell and Michael P. McDonald, "Congress and America's Political Development: The Transformation of the Post Office from Patronage to Service," *American Journal of Political Science*, XLIII/3 (1999), pp. 792–811; Devin Leonard, *Neither Snow nor Rain: A History of the United States Postal Service*, reprint edn (New York, 2017).

6 Gifford, "Rural Americans, Postcards, and the Fiscal Transformation of the Post Office Department."

7 Daniel Gifford, "Golden Age of Postcards," www.saturdayeveningpost.com, December 12, 2016.

8 "The Postcard 'CRAZE,'" *The Times-Democrat* (New Orleans, Louisiana), January 2, 1909, p. 6.

9 Gifford, "Rural Americans, Postcards, and the Fiscal Transformation of the Post Office Department."

10 Ibid.

11 Ibid.

12 Christopher Browne, *Getting the Message: The Story of the British Post Office* (Stroud, 1993).

13 Fred Bassett, "Wish You Were Here! The Story of the Golden Age of Picture Postcards in the United States," www.nysl.nysed.gov, August 16, 2016.

14 "Oldest Postcard Sells for £31,750," www.bbc.com, March 8, 2002.

15 Frank Staff, *The Picture Postcard and Its Origins*, 1st edn (London, 1966), pp. 46–7.

16 Ibid., p. 84.

17 Ibid., p. 87.

18 Ibid., p. 53.

19 Ibid., p. 49.

20 "Postcard History," Smithsonian Institution Archives, https://siarchives.si.edu/history, September 19, 2013; Browne, *Getting the Message.*

21 Jason Farman, *Delayed Response: The Art of Waiting from the Ancient to the Instant World* (New Haven, CT, 2018).

22 Ibid., pp. 165–6; R. H. Mathews, "Message-sticks Used by the Aborigines of Australia," *American Anthropologist*, X/9 (1897), pp. 288–98.

23 Jason Farman, interview, February 11, 2020.

24 A. Leo Oppenheim, *Letters from Mesopotamia: Official, Business, and Private Letters on Clay Tablets from Two Millennia* (Chicago, IL, 1976).

25 Gerd Gropp, "The Development of a Near Eastern Culture during the Persian Empire," in *Mehregan in Sydney: Proceedings of the Seminar in Persian Studies During the Mehregan Persian Cultural Festival, Sydney, Australia 28 October–6 November 1994* (Sydney, 1998).

26 Leonard, *Neither Snow nor Rain*, pp. 5–6.

27 Lionel Casson, *Travel in the Ancient World* (Baltimore, MD, 1994).

28 Kenneth A. Wood, *Post Dates: A Chronology of Intriguing Events in the Mails and Philately* (Albany, NY, 1985), n.p.

29 Ibid.

30 Staff, *The Picture Postcard and Its Origins.*

31 Wood, *Post Dates.*

32 Staff, *The Picture Postcard and Its Origins*, p. 59.

33 Martyn Lyons, *Ordinary Writings, Personal Narratives: Writing Practices in 19th and Early 20th-century Europe* (Bern, 2007); Esther Milne, *Letters, Postcards, Email: Technologies of Presence* (New York, 2010).

34 As quoted in Staff, *The Picture Postcard and Its Origins*, p. 76.

35 Daniel Gifford, *American Holiday Postcards, 1905–1915: Imagery and Context* (Jefferson, NC, 2013), p. 1.

TWO THE MEANS OF MASS PRODUCTION

1 Walter Benjamin, *The Work of Art in the Age of Mechanical Reproduction* (London, 2008).

2 Celeste Olalquiaga, *The Artificial Kingdom: A Treasury of the Kitsch Experience*, 1st edn (New York, 1998), pp. 16–17.

3 Lydia Pyne, "Five Centuries of Play Between Word and Image," www.hyperallergic.com, October 10, 2018.

4 Colin H. Bloy, *A History of Printing Ink, Balls and Rollers, 1440–1850* (London, 1991), p. 1.

5 Ibid.

6 Ted Bishop, *The Social Life of Ink: Culture Wonder and Our Relationship with the Written Word* (Toronto, 2014), pp. 99–100.

7 Lydia Pyne, "A History of Ink in Six Objects," www.historytoday.com, May 16, 2018.

8 Bloy, *A History of Printing Ink, Balls and Rollers*, p. 98.

9 Mark Kurlansky, *Paper: Paging through History*, 1st edn (New York, 2017), p. 117.

10 Ibid.

11 Marissa Nicosia, interview, July 24, 2019.

12 Tessa Watt, *Cheap Print and Popular Piety, 1550–1640* (Cambridge, 1999), p. 11.

13 Ibid.

14 Ibid.

15 Ibid., p. 5.

16 Margaret Spufford, *Small Books and Pleasant Histories: Popular Fiction and Its Readership in Seventeenth-century England* (London, 1981), pp. 118–19.

17 Jeffrey L. Meikle, *Postcard America: Curt Teich and the Imaging of a Nation, 1931–1950* (Austin, TX, 2016); Ben Marks, "How Linen Postcards Transformed the Depression Era Into a Hyperreal Dreamland," www.collectorsweekly.com, accessed January 29, 2016.

18 "The Postcard 'CRAZE,'" *The Times-Democrat* (New Orleans, LA), January 2, 1909, p. 6.

19 Watt, *Cheap Print and Popular Piety, 1550–1640*; Patricia Fumerton, Anita Guerrini and Kris McAbee, eds, *Ballads and Broadsides in Britain, 1500–1800*, 1st edn (Farnham, 2016).

20 Meikle, *Postcard America*, p. 3.

21 Ibid., p. 18.

22 Ibid., p. 29.

23 Phil Saunders, *Prints and Their Makers* (Princeton, NJ, 2020), p. 28.

24 Meikle, *Postcard America*; "MetroPostcard Guide to Postcard Printing Techniques 4," www.metropostcard.com, accessed April 11, 2020.

25 "Help Wanted, Female," *Chicago Daily Tribune*, September 11, 1906, p. 14.

26 "Help Wanted, Male," *Times Union* (Brooklyn, New York), April 23, 1910, p. 13; "Help Wanted, Male," *St. Louis Post-Dispatch* (St. Louis, MO), April 24, 1910, p. 2B.

27 Meikle, *Postcard America*, pp. 50–57.

28 Marks, "How Linen Postcards Transformed the Depression Era Into a Hyperreal Dreamland."

29 Ibid.

30 Ibid.

31 Meikle, *Postcard America*, p. 33.

32 Ibid., p. 32.

33 Ibid., p. 37.

34 Ibid., pp. 36–8.

35 Mark Simpson, "Postcard Culture in America," in *The Oxford History of Popular Print Culture* (Oxford, 2011), p. 179.

36 James N. Carder, "Curt Teich Co. Curteich–Chicago / C. T. American Art / C. T. Art–Colortone," www.doaks.org, accessed February 24, 2020.

37 Joni Hirsch Blackman, *This Used to Be Chicago* (St. Louis, MO, 2017), pp. 44–5.

38 "Curt Teich Postcard Archives Collection," www.newberry.org, accessed January 23, 2018.

39 Meikle, *Postcard America*, p. 465.

40 Blackman, *This Used to Be Chicago*, pp. 44–5.

41 "Postcards Offer Colorful Look at Historical Sites" *Argus-Leader* (Sioux Falls, SD), p. E3.

42 Quoted in Kurlansky, *Paper*, p. 98.

43 Janet Ing, "The Mainz Indulgences of 1454/5: A Review of Recent Scholarship," *British Library Journal*, IX/1 (1983), pp. 14–31.

45 Peter Stallybrass, "'Little Jobs': Broadsides and the Printing Revolution," in *Agent of Change: Print Cultural Studies after Elizabeth L. Eisenstein*, ed. Sabrina Alcorn Baron, Eric N. Lindquist, and Eleanor F. Shevlin (Cambridge, 2007), p. 316.

45 Ing, "The Mainz Indulgences of 1454/5."

46 Stallybrass, "'Little Jobs,'" p. 318.

47 Lydia Pyne, "Mapping Non-European Visions of the World," www.hyperallergic.com, August 14, 2019.

48 Mitch Fraas, interview, August 1, 2019.

THREE PUBLICITY AND PROPAGANDA

1 Roy Chapman Andrews, *Camps and Trails in China: A Narrative of Exploration, Adventure, and Sport in Little-known China*, 1st edn (Boston, MA, 1918), p. 75.

2 Kevin Coleman, *A Camera in the Garden of Eden: The Self-forging of a Banana Republic*, reprint edn (Austin, TX, 2016).

3 Garth Jowett and Victoria O'Donnell, *Propaganda and Persuasion*, 4th edn (Thousand Oaks, CA, 2006), p. 2.

4 Nicholas John Cull, David Holbrook Culbert, and David Welch, *Propaganda and Mass Persuasion: A Historical Encyclopedia, 1500 to the Present* (Santa Barbara, CA, 2003).

5 Ibid., p. xx.

6 "Real Photo Postcards: Collectors Weekly," www.collectorsweekly.com, accessed February 24, 2020.

7 "Kodaks Advertisements," *The Post-Star* (Glens Falls, New York), August 28, 1907, p. 8.

8 Paul J. Vanderwood and Frank Samponaro, *Border Fury: A Picture Postcard Record of Mexico's Revolution and U.S. War Preparedness, 1910–1917*, 1st edn (Albuquerque, NM, 1988), p. 3.

9 Rosamond B. Vaule, *As We Were: American Photographic Postcards, 1905–1930* (Boston, MA, 2004), p. 53.

10 Ibid., p. 189.

11 Ibid., p. 53.

12 "Kodak Finishing," *Evening Times-Republican* (Marshalltown, IA), May 20, 1913, p. 7; "Big Bear Studios Postcards, Views, Photo Postcards," *Los Angeles Evening Express,* 6 August 1919, p. 13;. "Furman's Studio Store: For Photographs, Enlarging, Kodak Finishing, etc.," *Norcatur Dispatch* (Norcatur, KS), 14 October 1920, p. 4.

13 Vaule, *As We Were*, p. 54.

14 "Kodaks Advertisements," p. 8.

15 Vaule, *As We Were*, p. 179.

16 "The Unfortunate Divorce of the Man Who Discovered Dinosaur Eggs," *Santa Fe New Mexican*, July 29, 1931; Lydia Pyne, "Yvette Borup Andrews: Photographing Central Asia," www.publicdomainreview.org, January 10, 2018.

17 Vaule, *As We Were*, p. 54.

18 Vanderwood and Samponaro, *Border Fury*, p. 6.

19 Vaule, *As We Were*, pp. 56–7.

20 Ibid., pp. 58–9.

21 Vanderwood and Samponaro, *Border Fury*, p. 13.

22 "Instagram by the Numbers (2020): Stats, Demographics and Fun Facts," January 26, 2020, www.omnicoreagency.com.

23 Vanderwood and Samponaro, *Border Fury*.

24 Ibid., p. 60.

25 Kenneth Florey, *Women's Suffrage Memorabilia: An Illustrated Historical Study* (Jefferson, NC, 2013); "Suffrage Campaign Propaganda. Work of Kardos, Boske," www.digitalcollections,nypl.org, accessed October 27, 2020; Kenneth Florey, *American Woman Suffrage Postcards: A Study and Catalog* (Jefferson, NC, 2015).

26 Vanderwood and Samponaro, *Border Fury*, p. 5.

27 Kenneth Florey, *Women's Suffrage Memorabilia*, p. 9.

28 Florey, *American Woman Suffrage Postcards*.

29 Ibid., p. 109.

30 Florey, *Women's Suffrage Memorabilia*, pp. 140–41.

31 Georgina Tomlinson, "The Suffrage Movement," www.postalmuseum.org, February 6, 2018.

32 Catherine H. Palczewski, "The Male Madonna and the Feminine Uncle Sam: Visual Argument, Icons, and Ideographs in 1909 Anti-woman Suffrage Postcards," *Quarterly Journal of Speech*, XCI/4 (November 1, 2005), pp. 365–94.

33 Vaule, *As We Were*, p. 19.

FOUR HAVING A WONDERFUL TIME, WISH YOU WERE HERE

1 Celia K. Corkery and Adrian J. Bailey, "Lobster Is Big in Boston: Postcards, Place Commodification, and Tourism," *GeoJournal*, XXXIV/4 (1994), pp. 491–8.

2 Rudy Koshar, "'What Ought to Be Seen': Tourists' Guidebooks and National Identities in Modern Germany and Europe," *Journal of Contemporary History*, XXXIII/3 (1998), pp. 323–40, p. 339.

3 Corkery and Bailey, "Lobster Is Big in Boston," p. 491.

4 Jean-Christophe Foltête and Jean-Baptiste Litot, "Scenic Postcards as Objects for Spatial Analysis of Tourist Regions," *Tourism Management*, 49 (August 2015), pp. 17–28, p. 18.

5 A. Leo Oppenheim, *Letters from Mesopotamia: Official, Business, and Private Letters on Clay Tablets from Two Millennia* (Chicago, IL, 1976), p. 74.

6 Lionel Casson, *Travel in the Ancient World* (Baltimore, MD, 1994), p. 23.

7 Jason Farman, *Delayed Response: The Art of Waiting from the Ancient to the Instant World* (New Haven, CT, 2018).

8 Christopher Deakes, *A Postcard History of the Passenger Liner* (Mystic, CT, 1970), p. 14.

9 Ibid., p. 19.

10 Paul J. Vanderwood and Frank Samponaro, *Border Fury: A Picture Postcard Record of Mexico's Revolution and U.S. War Preparedness, 1910–1917*, 1st edn (Albuquerque, NM, 1988).

11 Deakes, *A Postcard History of the Passenger Liner*, p. 17.

12 "How Do I Mail a Postcard While on a Cruise to the Bahamas?," www.traveltips.usatoday.com, accessed February 24, 2020.

13 Allison C. Marsh, "Greetings from the Factory Floor: Industrial Tourism and the Picture Postcard," *Curator: The Museum Journal*, LI/4 (2008), pp. 377–91, p. 377.

14 Koshar, "'What Ought to Be Seen,'" p. 323.

15 Kathleen Sheppard, interview, July 19, 2019.

16 Eric Zuelow, *A History of Modern Tourism*, 1st edn (London, 2015), p. 79.

17 Sonja Pyne, *Leon and the Colonel: Leon Noel Stuart, Joseph A. Robertson and Their Quest for Citrus and a Railroad* (Glendale, CA, 2013).

18 Melody Schreiber, "The Surprising History Of Old-timey Swahili Postcards," www.npr.org, June 10, 2018.

19 Ibid.

20 Mahima A. Jain, "Racism and Stereotypes in Colonial India's 'Instagram,'" www.bbc.com, September 30, 2018; "From Madras to Bangalore: Picture Postcards as Urban History of Colonial India: Brunei Gallery Exhibition: SOAS University of London," www.soas.ac.uk, accessed September 30, 2018.

21 Ibid.

22 Nicola Williams, *Lonely Planet France* (Melbourne, 2019), p. 587.

23 Lydia Pyne, "Resetting the Clock," www.historytoday.com, February 2, 2020.

24 Charles Simic, "The Lost Art of Postcard Writing," www.theguardian.com, August 4, 2011.

25 "Mali Travel Advisory," www.travel.state.gov, accessed February 24, 2020.

26 Clair MacDougall, "Why It's Easy—and Hard—to Get a Postcard All the Way from Timbuktu," www.npr.org, September 22, 2018.

27 "Postcards from Timbuktu," www.postcardsfromtimbuktu.com, accessed September 22, 2020.

28 "Postcards from Timbuktu on Instagram: 'A New Batch of Postcards Has Just Arrived from #Timbuktu. Now the Second Part of Their Journey Begins. They've Already Been on 3 Different . . .,'" www.instagram.com, accessed February 24, 2020.

FIVE POSTCARDS FROM COUNTRIES THAT NO LONGER EXIST

1 Les Harding, *Dead Countries of the Nineteenth and the Twentieth Centuries: Aden to Zululand* (Lanham, MD, 1998), p. vii.

2 Nick Middleton, *An Atlas of Countries That Don't Exist: A Compendium of Fifty Unrecognized and Largely Unnoticed States* (New York, 2001), p. 12.

3 Benedict Anderson, *Imagined Communities: Reflections on the Origin and Spread of Nationalism*, revd edn (London, 2016), p. 67.

4 Bjørn Berge, *Nowherelands: An Atlas of Vanished Countries, 1840–1975* (London, 2017), p. 8.

5 Alison Rowley, *Open Letters: Russian Popular Culture and the Picture Postcard, 1880–1922* (Toronto, 2013), p. 4.

6 Ibid.

7 Ibid.; Tobie Mathew, *Greetings from the Barricades: Revolutionary Postcards in Imperial Russia* (London, 2019).

8 Verlag Karl Baedeker, *Russia with Teheran, Port Arthur, and Peking* (Leipzig, 1914), p. 454.

9 Mathew, *Greetings from the Barricades*, p. 23.

10 Ibid., p. 48

11 Ibid., p. 45.

12 Alison Rowley, interview, February 3, 2020.

13 Tobie Mathew, "Postcards and the Russian Revolution," www.historytoday.com, February 2, 2019.

14 Mathew, *Greetings from the Barricades*, p. 24.

15 Mathew, "Postcards and the Russian Revolution."

16 Nicholas V. Riasanovsky, *A History of Russia*, 5th edn (New York, 1993), pp. 406–7.

17 Mathew, "Postcards and the Russian Revolution."

18 Rowley, *Open Letters*, p. 201.

19 Ibid., p. 238.

20 Riasanovsky, *A History of Russia*, p. 225.

21 Rowley, *Open Letters*, p. 11.

22 "A Russian Post-card," *Middletown Transcript* (Middleton, Delaware), June 30, 1917, p. 8.

23 Rowley, *Open Letters*, p. 7.

24 Mathew, *Greetings from the Barricades*.

25 Jessica Cline, interview, October 31, 2019.

26 Ibid.

27 Jay Vissers, interview, October 31, 2019.

28 "Holiday Postcards: NYPL Digital Collections," www.digitalcollections.nypl.org, accessed February 24, 2020.

29 Vissers, interview.

30 Cline, interview.

31 Samuel M. Blekhman, *The Postal History and Stamps of Tuva*, ed. J. Eric Slone, trans. Ron Hogg (Woodbridge, VA, 1997), p. 5.

32 Middleton, *An Atlas of Countries That Don't Exist*, p. 17.

33 Cline, interview.

34 Anja Mutic, "'I'm from a Country That No Longer Exists,'" www.bbc.com, April 26, 2016.

35 Vissers, interview.

CONCLUSION: THE AFTERLIVES OF POSTCARDS

1 "Six Postcards from Famous Writers: Hemingway, Kafka, Kerouac & More," *Open Culture* (blog), March 7, 2013.

2 Sheila Liming, email interview, June 10, 2019.

3 "Post Card Albums!" *Huntington Herald* (Huntington, IN), August 21, 1909, p. 2.

4 Frank Staff, *The Picture Postcard and Its Origins*, 1st edn (London, 1966); Martin Willoughby, *A History of Postcards: A Pictorial Record from the Turn of the Century to the Present Day* (London, 1994).

5 Jeremy Cooper, *Artists' Postcards: A Compendium*, reprint edn (London, 2015).

6 Erin Thompson, *Possession: The Curious History of Private Collectors from Antiquity to the Present* (New Haven, CT, 2016), p. 1.

7 Kenneth Florey, *American Woman Suffrage Postcards: A Study and Catalog* (Jefferson, NC, 2015), p. 5.

8 "Oldest Postcard Sells for £31,750," www.bbc.com, March 8, 2002.

9 Carolyn Kellogg, "Newly Discovered Jack Kerouac Letters to Be Auctioned," www.latimes.com, September 15, 2014.

10 "Jack the Ripper Postcard Sold for £22,000 at Auction," www.bbc.com, April 30, 2018.

11 "300 Rare Artists' Postcards Go on Show at the British Museum," www.artdaily.com, accessed August 28, 2019.

12 Thompson, *Possession*, p. 1.

13 Brian Lund, *Picture Postcard Monthly*, phone interview, April 27, 2020.

14 "Postcards to Voters," www.postcardstovoters.org, accessed April 21, 2020.

15 Suzanne Bloom and Ed Hill, phone interview, April 16, 2020.

16 "Zoe Leonard: Survey," www.whitney.org, accessed March 9, 2018; Zoe Leonard, *Zoe Leonard: You see I am here after all* (New York, 2011).

BIBLIOGRAPHY

....

Anderson, Benedict, *Imagined Communities: Reflections on the Origin and Spread of Nationalism*, revd edn (London, 2016)

Andrews, Roy Chapman, *Camps and Trails in China: A Narrative of Exploration, Adventure, and Sport in Little-known China*, 1st edn (Boston, 1918)

Bassett, Fred, "Wish You Were Here! The Story of the Golden Age of Picture Postcards in the United States," www.nysl.nysed.gov, accessed August 16, 2016

Benjamin, Walter, *The Work of Art in the Age of Mechanical Reproduction* (London, 2008)

Berge, Bjørn, *Nowherelands: An Atlas of Vanished Countries, 1840–1975* (London, 2017)

Bishop, Ted, *The Social Life of Ink: Culture Wonder and Our Relationship with the Written Word* (Toronto, 2014)

Blackman, Joni Hirsch, *This Used to Be Chicago* (St. Louis, MO, 2017)

Blekhman, Samuel M., *The Postal History and Stamps of Tuva*, ed. J. Eric Slone, trans. Ron Hogg (Woodbridge, VA, 1997)

Bloy, Colin H., *A History of Printing Ink, Balls and Rollers, 1440–1850* (London, 1991)

Browne, Christopher, *Getting the Message: The Story of the British Post
Office* (Stroud, 1993)

Carder, James N., "Curt Teich Co. Curteich-Chicago / C. T. American
Art / C. T. Art-Colortone," www.doaks.org, accessed February 24,
2020

Casson, Lionel, *Travel in the Ancient World* (Baltimore, MD, 1994)

Coleman, Kevin, *A Camera in the Garden of Eden: The Self-forging
of a Banana Republic*, reprint edn (Austin, TX, 2016)

Cooper, Jeremy, *Artists' Postcards: A Compendium*, reprint edn
(London, 2015)

Corkery, Celia K., and Adrian J. Bailey, "Lobster Is Big in Boston:
Postcards, Place Commodification, and Tourism," *GeoJournal*,
XXXIV/4 (1994), pp. 491–8

Croft, Jennifer, "Notes on Postcards," www.lareviewofbooks.org,
accessed October 11, 2020

Cull, Nicholas John, David Holbrook Culbert, and David Welch,
*Propaganda and Mass Persuasion: A Historical Encyclopedia, 1500
to the Present* (Santa Barbara, CA, 2003)

Deakes, Christopher, *A Postcard History of the Passenger Liner* (Mystic,
CT, 1970)

Farman, Jason, *Delayed Response: The Art of Waiting from the Ancient
to the Instant World* (New Haven, CT, 2018)

Florey, Kenneth, *American Woman Suffrage Postcards: A Study and
Catalog* (Jefferson, NC, 2015)

——, *Women's Suffrage Memorabilia: An Illustrated Historical Study*
(Jefferson, NC, 2013)

Foltête, Jean-Christophe, and Jean-Baptiste Litot, "Scenic Postcards
as Objects for Spatial Analysis of Tourist Regions," *Tourism
Management*, 49 (August 2015), pp. 17–28

Fumerton, Patricia, Anita Guerrini, and Kris McAbee, eds, *Ballads
and Broadsides in Britain, 1500–1800*, 1st edn (Farnham, 2016)

Gifford, Daniel, *American Holiday Postcards, 1905–1915: Imagery and
Context* (Jefferson, NC, 2013)

——, "Golden Age of Postcards," www.saturdayeveningpost.com, December 12, 2016

——, "Rural Americans, Postcards, and the Fiscal Transformation of the Post Office Department, 1909–1911," in *The Winton M. Blount Postal History Symposia: Selected Papers, 2010–2011* (Washington, DC, 2012)

Gropp, Gerd, "The Development of a Near Eastern Culture during the Persian Empire," in *Mehregan in Sydney: Proceedings of the Seminar in Persian Studies During the Mehregan Persian Cultural Festival, Sydney, Australia 28 October–6 November 1994* (Sydney, 1998)

Harding, Les, *Dead Countries of the Nineteenth and the Twentieth Centuries: Aden to Zululand* (Lanham, 1998)

"Holiday Postcards—NYPL Digital Collections," www.digitalcollections.nypl.org, accessed February 24, 2020

Ing, Janet, "The Mainz Indulgences of 1454/5: A Review of Recent Scholarship," *British Library Journal*, IX/1 (1983), pp. 14–31

Jain, Mahima A., "Racism and Stereotypes in Colonial India's 'Instagram,'" www.bbc.com, September 30, 2018

Jowett, Garth, and Victoria O'Donnell, *Propaganda and Persuasion*, 4th edn (Thousand Oaks, CA, 2006)

Kernell, Samuel, and Michael P. McDonald, "Congress and America's Political Development: The Transformation of the Post Office from Patronage to Service," *American Journal of Political Science*, XLIII/3 (1999), pp. 792–811

Koshar, Rudy, "'What Ought to Be Seen': Tourists' Guidebooks and National Identities in Modern Germany and Europe," *Journal of Contemporary History*, XXXIII/3 (1998), pp. 323–40

Kurlansky, Mark, *Paper: Paging through History*, 1st edn (New York, 2017)

Leonard, Devin, *Neither Snow nor Rain: A History of the United States Postal Service*, reprint edn (New York, 2017)

Lyons, Martyn, *Ordinary Writings, Personal Narratives: Writing Practices in 19th and Early 20th-century Europe* (Oxford, 2007)

Marks, Ben, "How Linen Postcards Transformed the Depression Era into a Hyperreal Dreamland," www.collectorsweekly.com, accessed January 29, 2016

Marsh, Allison C., "Greetings from the Factory Floor: Industrial Tourism and the Picture Postcard," *Curator: The Museum Journal*, LI/4 (2008), pp. 377–91

Mathew, Tobie, *Greetings from the Barricades: Revolutionary Postcards in Imperial Russia* (London, 2019)

——, "Postcards and the Russian Revolution," www.historytoday.com, February 2, 2019

Mathews, R. H., "Message-sticks Used by the Aborigines of Australia," *American Anthropologist*, X/9 (1897), pp. 288–98

Meikle, Jeffrey L., *Postcard America: Curt Teich and the Imaging of a Nation, 1931–1950* (Austin, TX, 2016)

Middleton, Nick, *An Atlas of Countries That Don't Exist: A Compendium of Fifty Unrecognized and Largely Unnoticed States* (New York, 2001)

Milne, Esther, *Letters, Postcards, Email: Technologies of Presence* (New York, 2010)

Olalquiaga, Celeste, *The Artificial Kingdom: A Treasury of the Kitsch Experience*, 1st edn (New York, 1998)

Oppenheim, A. Leo, *Letters from Mesopotamia: Official, Business, and Private Letters on Clay Tablets from Two Millennia* (Chicago, IL, 1976)

Palczewski, Catherine H., "The Male Madonna and the Feminine Uncle Sam: Visual Argument, Icons, and Ideographs in 1909 Anti-woman Suffrage Postcards," *Quarterly Journal of Speech*, XLI/4 (November 1, 2005), pp. 365–94

Parr, Martin, *Boring Postcards* (London, 2004)

Pyne, Lydia, "Five Centuries of Play Between Word and Image," www.hyperallergic.com, October 10, 2018

——, "A History of Ink in Six Objects," www.historytoday.com, May 16, 2018

——, "Mapping Non-European Visions of the World,"
www.hyperallergic.com, August 14, 2019

——, "Resetting the Clock" www.historytoday.com, February 2, 2020

——, "Yvette Borup Andrews: Photographing Central Asia,"
www.publicdomainreview.org, January 10, 2018

Pyne, Sonja, *Leon and the Colonel: Leon Noel Stuart, Joseph A. Robertson and Their Quest for Citrus and a Railroad* (Glendale, AZ, 2013)

"Real Photo Postcards," www.collectorsweekly.com, accessed February 24, 2020

Riasanovsky, Nicholas V., *A History of Russia*, 5th edn (New York, 1993)

Rowley, Alison, *Open Letters: Russian Popular Culture and the Picture Postcard, 1880–1922*, 1st edn (Toronto, 2013)

Sanders, Phil, *Prints and Their Makers* (Princeton, NJ, 2020)

Simic, Charles, "The Lost Art of Postcard Writing," www.theguardian.com, August 4, 2011

Simpson, Mark, "Postcard Culture in America," in *The Oxford History of Popular Print Culture* (Oxford, 2011), pp. 169–89

Smithsonian Institution Archives, "Postcard History,"
https://siarchives.si.edu, September 19, 2013

Spufford, Margaret, *Small Books and Pleasant Histories: Popular Fiction and Its Readership in Seventeenth-century England* (London, 1981)

Staff, Frank, The *Picture Postcard and Its Origins*, 1st edn (London, 1966)

Stallybrass, Peter, "'Little Jobs': Broadsides and the Printing Revolution," in *Agent of Change: Print Cultural Studies after Elizabeth L. Eisenstein*, ed. Sabrina Alcorn Baron, Eric N. Lindquist, Eleanor F. Shevlin (Cambridge, 2007)

Thompson, Erin, *Possession: The Curious History of Private Collectors from Antiquity to the Present*, 1st edn (New Haven, CT, 2016)

Todd, Michael, "A Short History of Home Mail Delivery,"
www.psmag.com, February 6, 2013

Tolentino, Jia, "The Age of Instagram Face," www.newyorker.com, accessed February 24, 2020

Vanderwood, Paul J., and Frank Samponaro, *Border Fury: A Picture Postcard Record of Mexico's Revolution and U.S. War Preparedness, 1910–1917*, 1st edn (Albuquerque, NM, 1988)

Vaule, Rosamond B., *As We Were: American Photographic Postcards, 1905–1930* (Boston, MA, 2004)

Watt, Tessa, *Cheap Print and Popular Piety, 1550–1640* (Cambridge, 1999)

Willoughby, Martin, *A History of Postcards: A Pictorial Record from the Turn of the Century to the Present Day* (London, 1994)

Wood, Kenneth A., *Post Dates: A Chronology of Intriguing Events in the Mails and Philately* (Albany, NY, 1985)

Zuelow, Eric, *A History of Modern Tourism*, 1st edn (London, 2015)

ACKNOWLEDGMENTS

. . . .

Postcards is a book about social networks, and I couldn't have written such a book without the time, interest, expertise, and enthusiasm of my colleagues, friends, family, and other researchers. I owe a huge debt to: Suzanne Bloom, James Burnes, Andrew Clayman, Jessica Cline, Kat Escher, Jason Farman, Mitch Fraas, Todd Fuller, Daniel Gifford, Ed Hill, Raymond Khan, Sheila Liming, Brian Lund, Courtney Meador, Joan Neuberger, Marissa Nicosia, Megan Raby, Alison Rowley, Kathleen Sheppard, Jay Vissers, and Liliane Weissberg.

Many institutions have been kind enough to open their postcard collections to my queries and to facilitate my research: Institute of Historical Studies (University of Texas at Austin), Interlibrary Loan and librarians (University of Texas at Austin), and most especially the New York Public Library Picture Collection. Holly Zemsta graciously shared her thoughts on many early drafts. My editor, Vivian Constantinopoulos, has helped turn this project from idea to book. As managing editor, Martha Jay saw this project through its production.

Over the past few years, my extended family—in particular Jetta Brewer Huber, Mauna Proctor, and Berthold and Marta Weinstein—have dug into their personal postcard collections to share their memories and bits of vacation ephemera with me for this project.

ACKNOWLEDGMENTS

One of the personal highlights of *Postcards* for me has been sending so very, very many postcards to my familial pen pals, and I love the weekly exchange of postcards with my grandmothers, Barbara Herrick and Guenavere Sandberg, and with my nieces and nephew, Ashley Brewer, Colten Brewer, Ivy Brewer, Julie Brewer, Karlie Brewer, and Lindsey Brewer. They have all eagerly shared their thoughts about postcards with me over the years. Special thanks go to Colten Brewer for his artwork contribution. My sister, Molly Pyne, was happy to bounce ideas around and dig into the question of postcards versus Instagram with me.

My parents, Steve and Sonja Pyne, have played no small role in my thinking about postcards. As a kid, postcards that my dad sent from his travels convinced me that the world was full of exciting, adventurous places to visit. I owe a massive debt to my mom, Sonja, as she curated and saved the family postcards discussed here and filled in the family history behind the collections. This book simply couldn't have been written without her contributions and expertise.

My daughter, Esther Pyne-Seibert, cheerfully mailed her first postcard—of what I'm sure will be many— to Grandma and Grandpa as I wrapped up editing this manuscript. And I am most grateful to Stan Seibert, for his appreciation of "the writing process," his keen interest in the topic, and his never-failing optimism that the book would actually get written.

PHOTO
ACKNOWLEDGMENTS

....

The author and publishers wish to express their thanks to the below sources of illustrative material and/or permission to reproduce it:

Bristol Archives: p. 156; courtesy of Andrew Clayman, Made in Chicago Museum, used with permission: pp. 65, 71, 72; Duke University Libraries Digital Collections, Durham, NC: p. 84; Library of Congress, Prints and Photographs Division, Washington, DC: pp. 16 (*foot*), 109, 128 (*foot*), 129 (*top*), 132, 141 (*right*), 165 (left), 176 (*top*), 177 (*foot*), 181; Los Angeles County Museum of Art (LACMA): p. 38; The Metropolitan Museum of Art, New York: p. 41; Musée Condé, Chantilly: p. 79; National Postal Museum, Curatorial Photographic Collection, Smithsonian Institution, Washington, DC: p. 22; The Newberry Library, Chicago, IL: p. 81; The New York Public Library: pp. 20, 76, 88, 90, 96, 125, 129 (*foot*), 136, 144, 200; private collection: pp. 8, 12, 13, 25, 28, 29, 36, 48 (*foot*), 49, 53, 97, 100, 103, 104, 116, 121, 124, 137, 140, 149, 180, 184 (*foot*), 189, 192, 197, 201; photo Lydia Pyne: p. 173; courtesy of Alison Rowley: pp. 161, 165 (*right*), 166, 167, 168; from Hans Sachs, *Eygentliche Beschreibung aller Stände auff Erden, hoher und niedriger, geistlicher und weltlicher, aller Künsten, Handwerken und Händeln* (Frankfurt, 1568): p. 52; Wikimedia Commons: pp. 9 (Newberry Library), 16 (Thmsfrst, *top*), 32 (Kürschner/norsemann_de), 44 (Sporti),

48 (Newberry Library, *top*), 68 and 69 (Newberry Library), 93 (from The Pulp Magazine Archive), 112 and 113 (People's History Museum, Manchester), 120 (Newberry Library), 127 (Missouri Historical Society, St Louis, *top*), 133 (Manfred Heyde, CC BY-SA 3.0), 141 (collection of Clare Harris, *left*), 153 (Arno-nl), 160 (Sijtze Reurich, CC BY-SA 4.0), 164 (Vladimir Lobachev), 169 (A. Sdobnikov), 176 (DarwIn, *foot*), 177 (Cornell University Library, Ithaca, NY, *top*), 184 (Silent Otto, *top*), 203 (Wikiolo, CC BY-SA 4.0).

INDEX

....

Page numbers in *italics* refer to illustrations

Abercrombie & Fitch Co. 92
American Museum of Natural
    History 83, 85
Anderson, Benedict 154
Andrews, Yvette Borup 83–6, 90,
    92–3, 99, 114
anti-suffrage movement 111–13
    see also suffrage movement
Antiques Roadshow 50
Austria-Hungary 17, 33

Baedeker guidebook 131, *133*, 159
ballads 59–60
Bassett, Fred 26
Benjamin, Walter 54
Berge, Bjørn 157
Bloy, Colin 55–7
Boles, Robert 12, 14, 25–6, 30, 35,
    116, 122, 134

Boston 115, 117
British Museum 194–5
broadsides 59–60
Bryant, Katherine 95, 97

camera
    Graflex 85, 100, 114
    Graphic 85
    Kodak 3A *84*, 85, 87, 89, 91,
        100, 114
carte postale 17, 145, 196
Cline, Jessica 175, 181, 185
colonialism 26, 139–40, 142, 152,
    154–5, 157, 179, 182
    British Empire 139–42, 152–4,
        156–7, 179
Cooper, Jeremy 194–5
Correspondenz-Karten 16, 17, 31
Crimea 152, 154–5, 183

cuneiform tablets *38*, 39–40, 47, 118–19, 130
Curt Teich & Co. 11, 34, 51–5, 61–75, 80, 87, 101, 187, 196
    linen-like cardstock 72–3
    postcards, examples *9, 53, 61, 69, 71–2, 76*
    see also lithography, offset
Curt Teich Archives Collection 51, 74–5

Darius, ruler of Persia 42, 46
dead countries 152, 155, 157–8, 172, 182–3, 186
Deakes, Christopher 125–6
Detroit Publishing Company 53, 64
Diamond Post Card Gun 95

Edward IV, king of England 45

Farman, Jason 37, 38
Field Post Cards 34
Florey, Kenneth 110, 192
Fouquet, Jean, *La Descente du Saint-Esprit* (photo reproduction) *41*

Georgian Military Road 159, *165–7, 181*
Germany 33, 44–5, 53, 62–6, 74, 77, 126, 131, 155, 157
Gifford, Daniel 15, 19, 24
Golden Age of Postcards 14, 27
Gutenberg, Johannes *52*, 55, 57–8, 71, 77–8

Harding, Les 152
Harrington, John Walker 73–4
Herodotus 42
Herrmann, Emanuel 31
historical geography 152, 155, 171, 174–5, 179, 182
Holy Roman Empire 45
Hook, Theodore 31, 35, 42, 193
Horne, Walter H. 99–105, 114, 139, 162
Hugo, Victor 75

Imperial Penny Post Act 35
indulgences 77–8, *79*
Ing Freeman, Janet 78
ink 55–7, 63–4, 70–71, 77, 80
Instagram 11, 95, 97, 123, 146, 197, 203
    see also participatory media
Izvestiia Petrogradskogo Soveta 170

Jack the Ripper 194
Jones, Rosalie 108, 110

Kerouac, Jack 187–8, 193
Khan, Raymond 10, 175
Klein Postcard Service of Boston 115, 117
Kodak Eastman Company 85, 89–91, *93*, 94
Kodak Girls 94
Korrespondenzkarten 32, 33
Kurlansky, Mark 57–8

Lascaux 143, 145
Lenin, Vladimir *169*, 170
Leonard, Zoe 198–9
    You see I am here after all
    (2008) 198–9, *200*
Lund, Brian 195

mail delivery systems 21, 32–3,
    42–6
    see also postal systems
Marks, Ben 70
Marsh, Allison 130
Mathew, Tobie 163–4, 169
Meier, Prita 139–40, 142
Meikle, Jeffrey 53, 62, 64, 71, 75
Mesopotamia 118
message sticks, Aboriginal 37
messages
    preservation of 39, 58, 181, 196,
    201
    waiting for 9, 27, *29*, *36*, 37, *124*,
    196, 202
Metzger Post 44
Mexican Revolution 98–107, 126,
    139, 170
Mexican War Photo Postcard
    Company 101
Middleton, Nick 154–5, 185
Monterrey, Mexico *8*, *48*, 134–5,
    137, 138–9, *140*

nationalism 73, 78–9, 86, 98, 154,
    157, 162, 164, 171–2
New York Public Library Picture
    Collection 10, *173*–5, 178–9, 185

Niagara Falls 131, 198–9, *200*
Nicolas II, tsar of Russia *161*,
    167–*8*
Nicholas v, pope 77
Nineteenth Amendment 106,
    108
North Ingermanland 172
Notre-Dame 143, 145, 146

Olalquiaga, Celeste 54
открытое письмо ('open letters')
    17

Palczewski, Catherine 111, 113
Paleolithic 37
paper 57–8
participatory media 77–9, 87,
    108, 201
Payne-Aldrich Tariff 66
Penny Black stamp 31
Persia 39, 42–3, 151
Philip, king of Spain 78
pioneer cards 34, 106–7
Pitchford, G. I. 67, 70
Postal Museum 147
postal systems
    ancient Rome 43
    ancient Persia 42–3, 46
    Austria-Hungary 31
    empire, and 39, 43–6, 49
    Germany 17
    Middle Ages 44, 45
    see also mail systems
postcards from Timbuktu 147,
    148, *149*, 202

postcards
    afterlives 16–18, 188, 190, 195,
    197–9, 204
    American elections 17, 196–7,
    197
    circulating 196–9
    collecting 15, 171, 174, 190,
    191–8, *192*, 201
    colonialism 78–9, 139–42
    governmental regulations
    34–5, 158–9
    kitsch 54, 73, 130, 147, 183
    personal printing 93–5,
    99–100, 114
    real picture/real photo 87,
    92–3, *96–7*, 99–105, 110, 113–14,
    117, 170
    temporal markers, as 146, 157,
    171, 174, 186
    Velox 91–2
Postkarten 33
print
    disposable, cheap 59–61, 63
    halftone 64
    history of 55–8, 77–80, 92
    lithography 63–4, 66–7,
    162
    lithography, offset *65*, 66, 70
    mass production 26, 53–4,
    59, 70, 87, 107, 133, 201
    presses, history of 55–6
    see also Gutenberg, Johannes;
    participatory media
Private Mailing Card Act 34, 35
Private Mailing Cards 107

propaganda *13*, 34, 86, 97–8, 102,
    105, 111, 114, 134, 143
Prussia 34, 46

questionnaires 78–9

Raphael Tuck & Sons *48*, 30, 34,
    53, *81, 120*
Rochester Optical Company Post
    Card Printer 93, 94
Rowley, Alison 8, 158, 163, 170,
    172
Royal Mail 26, 45, 123, 127
Rural Free Delivery *22*, 22–3, 107
Russia
    Federation, Russian 154, 158,
    183
    Imperial 17, *153*, 157–72
Russian Revolution
    (1905) 167, 169
    (1917) 8, 160, 162, *164*, 174

Samponaro, Frank 89, 105, 107
scientific expeditions 83, 85, 86, *88*,
    92–3
Sheldon, Pavica 95, 96
Smithsonian's National Museum
    of African Art 139
social networks 12–18, 58, 61, 75,
    80, 95–7, 130, 143–55, 182,
    196–204
    contemporary social media
    11, 18
    see also Instagram;
    participatory media

Society of St Eugenia 159
Sonora News Co. 135, 138
souvenirs 17, 63, 92, 106–8, 117–18, 130, 142, *189*, 203
Spanish-American War 19
Staff, Frank 33, 47
Stallybrass, Peter 78, 80
Stratton, H. H. 103, 105
Stuart, Mary Virginia 134–5, 138
suffrage movement 105–8, 111–13
    in UK 105–6, 110, *112–13*
    in U.S. 105–6, 108–10, *109*, 112
    see also anti-suffrage movement

Tannu Tuva *180*, 182–3
tarjeta postal 135, *137*, 138
tourism
    digital 148
    expectations of *44*, 116–17, *116*, 135, 139–40, *141*, 175, 181–2, *184–5*, 196, 202
    history of 118–19, 122–3
    performativity of 116–19, 123, 127, 131, *132*, *136*
    see also travel; Twain, Mark
transportation
    airplane 148
    horse 44, 138
    packet boat 46

passenger liner 123, *125*, 126, *128–9*
    pedestrian 42, 46
    railroad 122, 138
travel 119, 122, 125
    see also tourism
Treaty of Bern 33, 159
Twain, Mark 117, *120*, 190

Ukraine 154, 183
United Nation membership 155
United States Post Office 19–24, 27, 34, 47, 50, 117
    financial crisis of 1909 19, *20*, *25*, 27, *28–9*, 30, 47, 66, 117, 191
Universal Postal Union 33, 159
USSR 158, 162–3, 170–72, 182–3
Uzbekistan *184*

Vanderwood, Paul 89, 103, 107
Vaule, Rosamond 89, 90, 114
Victoria, queen of the UK 159
Villa, Pancho 102
Vissers, Jay 175, 178, 185
von Taxis, Johann 45

Welch, David 86–7
Wharton, Edith 188, 190

Yongle Emperor 45